Becoming a Director

Becoming a Director

Learn the basics and become an
effective and successful director

Victor Hughes

howtobooks

Published by How To Books Ltd,
3 Newtec Place, Magdalen Road,
Oxford OX4 1RE. United Kingdom.
Tel: (01865) 793806. Fax: (01865) 248780.
email: info@howtobooks.co.uk
http://www.howtobooks.co.uk

British Library Cataloguing in Publication Data
A catalogue record for this book is available from the British Library

Produced for How To Books by Deer Park Productions, Tavistock
Typeset by PDQ Typesetting, Newcastle-under-Lyme, Staffs.
Edited by Francesca Mitchell
Cover design by Baseline Arts Ltd, Oxford
Printed and bound in Great Britain by Bell & Bain Ltd, Glasgow

NOTE: The material contained in this book is set out in good faith for general guidance and no liability
can be accepted for loss or expense incurred as a result of relying in particular circumstances on
statements made in the book. The laws and regulations are complex and liable to change, and readers
should check the current position with the relevant authorities before making personal arrangements.

Contents

Foreword

It has always amazed me that people think being appointed a director is a great honour and the ultimate accolade in business. In my experience people rush to accept a directorship and rarely understand what it entails; the responsibilities and the liabilities.

Thank goodness that now there is a sensible publication that explains what to do before accepting and whilst one is a director. Victor Hughes has produced a common-sense book that will be of great assistance to directors. It s full of practical assistance and without any waffle.

I have had the privilege to work with Victor in a number of countries and did know that he was a very good practical teacher on governance issues. However, I did not know, and am now delighted to attest to the fact, that he can put this practical approach into a book, which I believe should be read by every aspiring and current director.

A board of directors is a collective consensus decision-making entity where the whole is far greater than the sum of the individuals. However, this collective can be destroyed, as I have witnessed, when one or some have no idea of the basics of directorship. Boards are there to add value for the shareholders and the stakeholders. This book can help directors focus on doing just that.

Geoffrey Bowes MNZM,
Chief Executive Commonwealth Association for
Corporate Governance

Introduction

Election to a Board of Directors often follows a successful career in a specialist area, finance, engineering or marketing; some directors may be practising professionals, while others may have retired from a full-time business career. After the sense of pride and pleasure at the invitation to join a board wears off, panic can take over. 'What does a director do? What have I let myself in for?'

Directors influence the fate of companies. Companies create much of the wealth of a country. It follows that directors must understand what their job entails. There are books listing a director's legal responsibilities; others detail all of the knowledge and abilities the ideal director should possess. Books like these can make those of us who are not able to fly faster than a speeding bullet or leap tall buildings with one bound seem somewhat inadequate.

A director's role is not fully or clearly defined. What definition exists, changes as a result of government studies and reports, court decisions, changes in law, criticism from shareholders, comments from politicians or guidelines issued by professional institutes, including institutes of directors. Perhaps this is as it should be, but it does make life difficult for a director.

None of these sources help a potential director decide whether to join a board, what questions need to be answered before reaching a decision, or how to do the job day by day. This book fills the gap. It is not a textbook on the laws and regulations surrounding directors nor does it advise on how to handle every specific situation. Laws are complex, company cultures differ, and companies even in the same industry are organised differently. This book is, incidentally, as relevant to 'not for profit' organisations as to commercial companies. Above all, 'directorship' involves people: each is an individual. The solution to a problem in corporate governance in one company may not work in another.

SO WHAT HAVE YOU GOT FOR YOUR MONEY?

This book will help potential and current directors, including those with the courtesy title, understand the fundamentals of a director's job. There is a discussion of companies and how they work, the information a director needs and how to operate, all illustrated with real examples. All of this will give directors the confidence to do their important job well.

The Chairman of one UK company commented that it is a year before a new director contributes positively to the working of his company. This book will help any new director play his part from the beginning.

When writing this book I have tried to avoid offending any person or group. My aim is to help, not irritate. Any references to the masculine apply equally to the feminine; the law does not make a distinction, nor do I. Details of some of the examples used have been changed to avoid the possibility of identifying individuals. The changes do not diminish the usefulness of the example. History is a good teacher.

ACKNOWLEDGEMENT

The publications of the Commonwealth Association for Corporate Governance, The Hong Kong Institute of Directors, Institute of Directors in New Zealand and the Institute of Directors in the UK have been a valuable source of information and guidance for this book. Thanks to the many people who have worked to produce the publications that help directors to understand their role. Thanks also to the Hong Kong Institute of Directors for agreeing that I could quote from their report 'Uniquely Hong Kong?'

The suggestion that I write this book came from Roger Carey of the International Business School on the Isle of Man. Now the book is in final form, I am grateful for his suggestion – there were times when I felt less than grateful.

My thanks to those who helped by providing information from around the world, Alastair MacAuley, David Newman, Ian Silver, Darcy Smith and Carlye Tsui. No jurisdiction has a monopoly on corporate governance guidance. It is useful to take a wide view.

Gerry Clemmow read and commented on an early draft of the book, making some very helpful comments. Not the least of which was confirmation that it would help 'new' directors. Thanks.

Hamish Masson encouraged me to write this book, confirming that there is a need to discuss the essentials of corporate governance issues. Hamish provided information, examples and made helpful suggestions on the content and layout of the book. Many thanks.

Geoffrey Bowes read the draft and made helpful and practical suggestions on each chapter. I appreciate the time and care. Thank you.

I am grateful to Jonathan Rice for his constructive comments and helpful advice throughout this project. I don't think that the book would have been finished without his encouragement and help.

My thanks to my wife, Helen, for her patience and support while I was writing the book, also for reading and commenting on each of the many drafts.

Everyone at How To Book has been sympathetic and positive and made the process of producing this book painless.

Why Become a Director, What's it All About?

'ABC Company Ltd would like you to join their Board of Directors.' A flattering invitation, but what is really involved?

The invitation may be to an executive of the company, to one of the company's advisors, to an individual who has useful experience or to the employee of a major shareholder. Regardless of background, the duties and responsibilities are the same for all directors.

What does the invitation mean? What do the specialist words used by companies and directors mean? To join the club it is necessary to understand the language.

Need a director worry about 'corporate governance'? You don't need to worry, but you should be aware of the need for good corporate governance and what it means, certainly. Corporate governance is not an area of threat to the majority of directors. Good corporate governance is essentially common sense exercised with integrity. There is plenty of guidance, but few rules.

WHAT IS A COMPANY?

A **limited liability company** is probably the most important driver of prosperity and growth ever invented. This way of organising an operation permits a venturist, a risk taker, to try to create wealth for himself and for others while limiting the amount that can be lost if the venture fails. The venture becomes a calculated risk. Limiting the potential for loss encourages an entrepreneur to try to build a business. There is frequent debate on the extent to which regulation limits a venturist's ability to create wealth and the need to legislate for integrity.

> **KEY POINT**
>
> A director, the guardian of the future of the company, is a vital part of the process of trying to create wealth and strengthening the national economy.

It is important to realise that a limited liability company is a separate legal entity (judicial person) that has limited liability and is separate from its founders and its shareholders. This separate legal existence comes from the process of its incorporation and can take a variety of forms. The two main types of incorporation are: companies limited by their share capital, which is by far the most common form, and companies limited by guarantee. Regardless of the form of incorporation, this separate legal entity has all the legal rights of a person to:

- conclude contracts
- employ staff
- borrow money
- operate a business.

Limited liability means that if the company fails, its shareholders only stand to lose the amount paid for the shares in the company plus any profits which the company has not paid out to them. Shareholders own some proportion of the company, often called a **share**, but they do not own the assets of the company. Evidence of ownership is usually a **share certificate** stating the number of shares or proportion of the company owned.

THE RESPONSIBILITIES OF SHAREHOLDERS AND DIRECTORS

The **shareholders** do not have the right to operate the company; the right to manage the company is vested in (possessed by) the company's Board of Directors. The shareholders pass over the responsibility for running the company to the directors.

Shareholders cannot make director's decisions for them, nor can they issue instructions to the Board. The shareholders are, however, able to rebuke the directors. The usual form of sanction is to:

◆ dismiss an individual or some or all directors
◆ appoint new directors
◆ liquidate the company or pass its management to administrators.

Directors have a duty to the company, to the separate legal entity; this is not a direct duty to the shareholders, but to the company. The directors are not the mandated delegates of the shareholders.

A meeting of the directors of a joint venture company was called to discuss a major problem. All directors agreed that a particular course was the best solution. A director, nominated to the Board by the largest shareholder, pointed out that the majority shareholder would prefer a different resolution; commenting that as the major shareholder owned the largest share of the company the board should do as the major shareholder wished, 'because it is their money'.

Clearly there is a problem in these circumstances because the director's duty is to protect the wellbeing of the company and in so doing benefit all of the shareholders, not to follow the instruction or recommendation of an individual, even the majority, shareholder.

This principle is enshrined in law in most jurisdictions, and is called a **fiduciary duty**, which is a duty 'given in trust'. Despite the importance of this duty it is not always remembered.

> At a conference a venture capital fund manager put forward the view that any person they nominate to the Board of a Company was there to represent the venture capitalist's interests. Not correct in law, but clearly even professional advisors do not necessarily know this.

Shareholders can lose their investment. Directors can also lose if they own shares.

Not enshrined in law, but generally accepted, is that a company also has obligations to those connected with it; frequently referred to as its **stakeholders**. These include its customers, employees, suppliers and the general community. This is discussed in more detail on page 148.

COMPANIES AND SUBSIDIARIES

Often another company, an **investor**, owns a large number of shares in a company. If the investor controls more than half of the voting rights in the Company and/or nominates the majority of the Board of Directors, that investor is called the **parent** and the company is its **subsidiary**. If an investor owns a significant number of shares in a company, but not enough to make it a subsidiary and is able to influence its management the company is called as *associate* of the investor.

These relationships can cause difficulties. The directors of the subsidiary have the same duties and responsibilities as in any other type of company. Even if nominated by the parent, they do not owe any special duty to the parent. If the management or directors of the parent attempt to make decisions for the subsidiary or influence the decisions of the subsidiary they become liable in the same way as the directors of the subsidiary.

There are practical ways to handle this problem. The Institute of Directors of New Zealand's *Best Practice Guide* advises that, if the constitution of the subsidiary expressly permits, a director of a subsidiary can act in the best interest of the investor, even if it is not in the best interests of the subsidiary:

- where the subsidiary is wholly owned

- where not wholly owned, with the prior agreement of the subsidiary's other shareholders.

This guidance only applies where the parent is a **holding company**, i.e. one formed to hold the shares of another company. New Zealand's laws acknowledge this situation and permits the practice.

A DIRECTOR'S FUNCTION

There is no single law or regulation completely defining the role a **Director** plays or what the duties and responsibilities are. Any 'definition' is spread between laws, court decisions and guidelines.

But the lack of a clear job description should not hold back an individual from becoming a director. Companies only look to the law for guidance to resolve disputes or conflicts. The law seeks to establish where the balance of benefit and right is held.

KEY POINT

A working definition of a Director is: 'An individual working with fellow directors to be collectively responsible for managing the affairs of a company to achieve its long-term prosperity by making the important decisions, monitoring performance and establishing ethical standards'.

A directorship should not be treated as a reward for those nearing the end of their career. A director is a member of the leadership team. Directorship is a human activity, difficult to define and changing with circumstances. There are guidelines for directors issued by various national institutes of directors which help a director understand what the job involves and how to do it well.

A DIRECTOR:

- ◆ is a statutory (legal) office in most jurisdictions.
- ◆ must use care and diligence when performing their duties – the same level of care and diligence a prudent person uses when managing their own affairs. Duties include setting objectives, monitoring performance and examining proposals.
- ◆ is expected to work with reasonable competence; there should not be any penalty for a simple error in judgement. A director is not expected to be infallible and is really only liable if there is a breach of duty.
- ◆ must act honestly, with integrity, taking appropriate care.

A director's responsibilities are quite separate from any position as a manager of the company or as a shareholder. There should not be any conflict between an executive director's managing duties and the wider responsibilities of the Board. All executive directors carry out their executive responsibilities within the framework of policies agreed by the Board. Difficulty may arise if the Board agrees a course of action that causes a problem in a particular department of the company, but each executive director must still work within Board agreed guidelines and follow decisions of the Board.

> The Board agreed that to conserve financial resources the company's cash outflow must be reduced significantly and permanently. Previously agreed amounts of capital expenditure were reduced. The executive director responsible for computer systems strongly argued for special treatment, but ultimately had to conform to the direction of the Board.

The day-to-day running of the company will be delegated by the directors to the company's managers, who are responsible for implementing the decisions and policies of the Board.

DIRECTORS' TITLES

Chairman
The **chairman** (sometimes called **chairperson** or **chair**) is a director and the 'leader of the gang', the leader of 'Team Board', responsible for managing the business of the Board, ensuring there is a balanced discussion of issues and that clear decisions are made – in all making sure that the Board works efficiently and effectively. It needs to be made clear that the chairman is not the chief executive of the

company unless the two roles are specifically combined. The current recommended best practice in most countries is that the chairman should not also be the chief executive.

> One professional chairman who chaired three separate public companies made it a rule never to meet the managing director more than once a month, except in emergency. However, he did keep in touch by phone almost every day to give advice, if it was asked for. This gave the managing director the help and advice he needed to run the business without the chairman interfering.

The chairman:

+ should lead the development of the company's strategy
+ acts as link between management and the Board
+ is responsible for overseeing the induction of new directors
+ chairs the meetings of shareholders, hence needs to know how to control what can be a large meeting.

Managing director

The leader of the management team is known as the **managing director** or **chief executive officer (CEO)** or some other similar title. The managing director or CEO should not also be the chairman of the Board, but sometimes is.

The reasons for recommending that the roles remain separate are:

+ One of the Board's roles is effectively to monitor the operation of the company's management; there is a difference in perspective, management deals with 'today' and its problems, the Board monitors 'today' and plans for 'tomorrow'.

♦ Having one person running the Board and the management team concentrates too much power in one person.

♦ There is the danger that the 'tyranny of the urgent' will highjack discussions of long-term issues, i.e. solving today's problem takes precedence over crafting plans for the future.

> A new managing director found many weighty capital expenditure proposals awaiting his approval, including property disposals that could affect the viability of the company. It was difficult to make decisions because there was no long-term strategic plan. He instituted and had agreed by the Board a long-term plan that formed the framework for making a decision on each proposal.

It may seem unnecessary for a company with limited operations, e.g. a company incorporated solely to manage the maintenance of a small block of flats, to separate duties. But the benefits of having a chairman acting as a mentor with a role separate from an executive managing director greatly outweigh any inconvenience; two heads are better than one when making a decision, even in a small operation!

Executive director

An **executive director** is a director who is also responsible for some part of a company's operations, i.e. a working employee. Each executive director should have a separate written contract of employment that will include a list of the executive's responsibilities.

Where an executive director is also the managing director, in addition to an employment contract there should be a statement of the powers the Board delegates to the managing director.

The number of executive and non-executive directors on a Board varies from company to company (see page 130), but when there are executive directors on the Board, one of them should be the chief executive officer.

An executive director at a Board meeting does not represent a particular part of the company, but is a director with the same full responsibilities as any other. The engineering director does not represent the engineering part of the business at a Board meeting and should not use the meeting to lobby a departmental interest. An executive director must support a Board's decision even though it conflicts with their department's interests.

> **The Board decided to close down several factories. The executive director responsible for the operations in the factories supported the Board's decision, but had then to return to his workplace to tell his colleagues that the operations were to be closed down.**

Those joining the Board of Directors should not be 'political' appointments. Difficulties can arise if the director seeks to represent the interest of the backers and not the interests of the company. Political appointees frequently do not understand the breadth of their responsibilities and may not be able to leave their other interests at the boardroom door. Failure to do so can be very disruptive to the workings of the company.

> A trade union appointee to the Board of an agricultural produce company viewed every Board decision in the light of the pay scales of his colleagues. Board decision-making became extremely difficult and the company suffered a series of strikes. In some countries this is a problem.

In developing countries it is common for major shareholders to be represented directly on the Board. Large companies and those in more developed economies tend to have a clearer separation between shareholders, even those with a large holding, and the Board. It is just the way economies develop.

Non-executive director

A **non-executive director** does not have any executive or management responsibility. In the USA the description **outside director** is often used. Every Board, whatever the size of the company, should have at least one non-executive director to provide an independent view on each matter discussed by the Board. A non-executive director can often see solutions that escape those who are close to a problem.

A non-executive director, however, has the same responsibilities as other directors and should know as much about the company's operation as the other directors. In practice it is difficult for a non-executive director to have the same level of knowledge as an executive because of their distance from operations. They also tend to receive information via the executives.

In some cases non-executive directors may already be giving other professional advice to the company. One study suggested that 80 per cent of non-executive directors were linked to the company in some way by contract or the provision of professional services by their firms. Given the potential for a conflict of interest this situation should be avoided. Hopefully the practice will become less prevalent.

Independent non-executive director

A non-executive director who does not have any relationship with a company other than as a director receiving directors' fees is an **independent non-executive director.** Independent means having an opinion that is not influenced by the desire for income, other than director's fees, from the company. The report produced by Derek Higgs in January 2003 for the UK government (Higgs Report) notes that there are 'over a dozen' definitions of independent non-executive director in the UK, 'all with different criteria'.

Countries have different ideas of what other income a non-executive director can earn from a company and remain independent. Some permit independent non-executive directors to receive income, other than director's fees, provided the amount is not 'significant'; others set a monetary limit, while still others prohibit earning any other income.

Many company annual reports note which directors the Board has determined are 'independent'.

The special contribution non-executive and independent non-executive directors make arises from their distance from the day-to-day decisions needed to run the company.

The status of directors

ALL DIRECTORS ARE EQUAL

None are more equal than others, regardless of title or specific responsibility.

The chairman, managing director (or chief executive officer), executive directors and non-executive directors are all equal, have the same duties and responsibilities and are all responsible for the leadership of the company. It is sometimes difficult for an executive director to accept this notion of equality, particularly when the chairman or chief executive officer set or influence their remuneration. Forming a remuneration committee will go some way to overcoming this difficulty.

Alternate director

An individual may be asked to become an **alternate director**, essentially a 'deputy director'. An alternate director is someone nominated by a director, empowered to perform the duties of that director, usually only at Board meetings, when the director is unable to attend. Alternate directors are often used in the UK and UK-orientated companies, particularly in joint-venture companies where the resolutions are passed by a majority 'of those directors attending' the board meeting.

In the UK this is a common practice on Boards in the 'not-for-profit' or public service areas. The alternate director may find it difficult to act adequately as a stand-in because they may not be fully briefed on the affairs of the company. The company's Articles of Association will state whether a director appointing an alternate is responsible for the alternate's actions. If the Articles are silent, the alternate will be responsible for their own actions. The ability to appoint an alternate director is usually provided by the Articles, not by law.

Company secretary

The **company secretary** is not a company director but is the chief administrative officer of the company and makes an important contribution to the smooth running of the Board, frequently acting as advisor to directors. The company secretary is the company's senior expert on company law, the company's own regulations and a vital reference point on corporate governance.

The company secretary's position varies country by country. In South Africa a company secretary can only be dismissed by the shareholders' meeting. New Zealand does not recognise that the position of company secretary exists at all!

Directors all?

There is a trend to give the courtesy title of 'Director' to departmental heads who do not have the power or responsibilities of a director on the Board.

This is a dangerous trend because it blurs responsibilities. Moreover, if the company ran into trouble and was investigated by regulatory authorities, courtesy directors could attract the same liabilities as a full member of the Board.

Directors are recognised by their function, authority and the power they exercise rather than their title. There may be individuals who are given the title **director**, **special director**, **local director**, **deputy director** or **divisional director** as a courtesy, although they do not join a company's Board of Directors nor exercise any of a director's duties. There is the danger that these individuals will be held responsible for the actions of the Board. However, if there is a problem the courts tend to apportion responsibility based on the influence an individual had on the decision(s) that produced the problem.

Similarly there is a danger to the company. If an individual appears to the outside world to be a director, the company could be bound by any contracts negotiated and agreed by the individual.

KEY POINT
Care is needed when granting the title 'Director'; it should only be given to those properly appointed and acting as a director and a voting member of the Board.

Shadow director

There may be those who are not directors of the company, but habitually give instructions on the direction of the company to the company's directors. These are **shadow directors** and have the same liability as a director. The name shadow director sounds sinister; any attempt to usurp the authority of the Board is sinister!

Investigations into the collapse of a major group of companies concluded that the largest shareholder and other individuals had acted as shadow directors, influencing the actions of other companies associated with the group.

Other titles

There are other titles in use and while there is nothing wrong with using them, a potential director and the outside world need to be clear what duties and authority each title carries. Some companies have a **chief operating officer** as well as a chief executive officer and this can create confusion; who is running the show?

Some Boards, often those with a high degree of family control, appoint a **president**, usually recognising an individual who has played a significant role in developing the company. Generally the individual would also be a director but where this is not the case, it is unclear whether the position of president has the same responsibilities as a director.

Strictly speaking, title is not important. A 'finance director' who attends Board meetings and votes on decisions is as much a director as a 'chief financial officer' who attends Board meetings and votes on decisions. Nevertheless, the cleanest way to operate is for each director to be called 'director' and for no-one else to use the title.

Some Boards have an **advisor**. This can also cause confusion; is the advisor a director or not? If an advisor attends Board meetings and takes part in discussions, there is the potential for the advisor to be considered a director.

If the Board needs the help of an advisor, but not another director, it would be better for the appointment to be made as advisor to the chairman and not attend Board meetings. If the Board needs the services of a group of advisors, they should be formed into an Advisory Committee or Panel with a clearly defined role that makes it clear that the advisors do not have any of the duties, responsibilities or authority of the directors.

If you are asked to become an advisor, it is important that the relationship with the Board is crystal clear. An advisor should take professional advice on the possibility of a claim of professional negligence arising from advice given and how to insure against any claim.

A similar problem arises when a general manager or other manager attends Board meetings. This is not uncommon. The Board needs to be careful; the manager should give information, but not be part of the decision making and should not vote on any matter. It is the responsibility of the chairman not to let the Board become uncontrollable.

If special advisors – for example, property advisors, technical advisers and legal advisors – need to brief the whole Board, then the correct procedure is to invite the advisors to join the meeting at the appropriate time, listen to the advice, ask the advisors to leave and then continue the Board meeting.

LOCAL CIRCUMSTANCES

Some countries and jurisdictions have special regulations or guidelines covering local circumstances. There are economies where it is common for a single family to be the largest shareholder and for family members to make up the majority of the Board of a company. To help protect the non-family shareholders, members of the same family should not hold more than half the voting rights on the Board. These special circumstances require particular care: directors need to remember when making decisions that their responsibility is to the company not to the family, and also that the role of the director is separate from the role of the shareholder and a manager.

In the UK these situations are less common. Any family influence tends to be modified by the attitude of the investing institutions and banks that support and invest in the company.

WHAT A BOARD DOES

When directors meet to discuss and decide on the affairs of the company, when they come together for decision making, they are described as the **Board of Directors.** A Board is a committee for making decisions.

The Board's overall role is to:

1. Define and articulate the objectives and strategies of the company.
2. Lay down policies and priorities.
3. Allocate resources, e.g. money, staff, production capacity.
4. Review, amend and approve company plans.
5. Monitor performance.
6. Ensure that the company remains solvent.

This list applies in all companies, regardless of the size of its operations. To illustrate, think of the workings of the Board of a small family-owned and operated company with, perhaps, two employees.

1. Define and articulate the objectives and strategies of the company

The answer to the question 'What is the long-term objective of running this business?' may range over:

'To have five or six shops in the area for our children to run when we retire.'

'I have always enjoyed making and repairing furniture; I want to earn a good living doing it and to retire when I reach 65.'

'We want to build a business to sell when we are 60, in 15 years time, so we can retire to the South of France.'

All of these are perfectly valid strategies and provide a clear framework for guiding business decisions.

2. Lay down policies and priorities

The statements of strategy above drive these items.

In the first case, the policy will be to build a long-term business and the priority will be to establish a number of shops.

For the second, the policy will be to specialise in quality furniture with the priority of maximising income.

For the third, the policy is to build a business, which will be worth a certain amount in 15 years, and the priority is to have a business that can be operated by a new buyer.

3. Allocate resources

Similarly, the strategy, policy and priorities guide the Board in how to allocate its funds and staff, and also where to focus operations.

4. Review, amend and approve company plans

Achieving the agreed objective will need a plan. Once there is an agreed plan it should be recorded and reviewed periodically. Changes may need to be considered depending on the progress made and whether the objective is still valid.

5. Monitor performance

Regularly the directors need to know what progress has been made towards achieving the agreed objective and also what the result of operating the business has been. A survey in the UK concluded that most small businesses prepare a budget for their results, but do not always compare actual performance against the budget.

6. Ensure that the company remains solvent

Every business must stay 'in business' if the goals are to be achieved. Each strategy requires that the business survive, to be passed on or sold. The directors need to monitor closely the finances of the business.

KEY POINT

The elements of a Board's role apply to all companies of whatever size.

Group decision making

The Board of Directors is a forum to share knowledge, experience and decisions on the assumption that a director's duties will be better carried out by a group than by an individual. Sadly, this does not always happen and there are many cases where Board decision making has been swayed, either by a dominant director or by 'closed-group thinking' or the tendency to defer to expertise.

Some years ago investors in a company lost their investment. One of the reasons given at the time was the tendency of Boards to accept without question the opinion of the expert members responsible for key operations. Very few people on the Board had the knowledge to question in detail the assumptions underlying the business plan suggested by the executive directors. Even if they did, very few directors were willing to ask such direct questions. It is essential that Boards have both the depth and breadth of experience and the willingness continually to evaluate their own activities.

The Board as a group does not have any separate responsibilities or duties from those of an individual director, but it is the forum where binding decisions are made.

The importance of a quorum

The Articles of Associations (internal regulations) of the company will establish the minimum number of directors who must be present at a Board meeting in order for decisions to be valid; this number is called a **quorum**. If a quorum is not present, valid decisions cannot be made.

> Two company chairmen, while playing golf, agreed to merge their two corporations. The shareholders subsequently called an Extraordinary General Meeting to challenge this decision on the basis that the original decision was not quorate (was made without a quorum). Not only did the shareholders win, they won substantial damages from both chairmen.

It is not uncommon now for directors to have the option to be present at a Board meeting 'electronically'. Essentially this means participating in the discussions and decisions by telephone. Personal experience has shown that this is not an easy option; long telephone calls with four or five other people can be very tiring. A more attractive option if you are not able to attend in person is to 'attend' the meeting through a video conferencing link.

Minutes of meetings

The decisions of all meetings of the Board of Directors and Board's sub-committees will be recorded; these records are called **minutes**. The minutes of the meetings may or may not detail all the discussions and arguments, but in all cases, the minutes must record clearly each decision made by the Board of Directors and who is responsible for implementing the decision.

COMPANY ORGANISATION

What can a company do, how is it organised? There is a definition of what businesses the shareholders have authorised the company to operate and rules about how the company is to be run. These are contained in the company's **Memorandum and Articles of Association,** also called **Company Memorandum of Incorporation and Articles of Association** or **Company Constitution.**

Memorandum of Association

The Memorandum of Association defines and lists the operations the company can perform. In some jurisdictions the list of operations will be very short and restrictive, in others the list will be long and include every possible operation the company might ever think of doing.

Articles of Association

The Articles of Association deal with how the company is organised at a high level, dealing with such matters as the procedure for appointing a director and the period of notice required to be given of the date and place of directors' meetings and shareholders' meetings. There is more detail on page 56.

The Articles of Association become important if there is a problem. If the Board finds that there are irreconcilable differences amongst directors, they will dust off a copy of the Articles of Association to determine what action and options are open to them, usually, if they are wise, with the advice of the company secretary.

Annual General Meeting

The directors are required to meet the shareholders at least once a year. This meeting has an agenda of standard items described in the Articles of Association. The meeting is called the **Annual General Meeting**.

Extraordinary General Meeting

The Articles of Association will provide for the possibility of meetings between shareholders and directors at other times to discuss important matters, e.g. a recommendation that the company stop trading or remove a director, or if a minority of shareholders is opposed to a major course of action such as a proposed merger. This type of meeting is called an **Extraordinary General Meeting**.

Related transactions

Depending on the country, either or both the Articles of Association or company law may restrict certain transactions between the company and its directors, such as prohibiting the company from a making a loan to a director.

Quite apart from related transactions between directors and the company, there is also the issue of a company's transactions with related parties within its own structure e.g. subsidiaries or associates as part of its day-to-day business. many business failures have revealed that worrying transactions were hidden by transactions between subsidiaries. a director needs to be alert to the unusual.

DUTIES

In a common law jurisdiction it is not possible to find a complete list of the legal duties of a director. The list changes in response to guidance from the national institute of directors, public pressure and as a result of court cases. A director's duties, in spirit, are to:

◆ always act honestly, in good faith in the best interest of the company, to meet the legitimate interests of the shareholders and stakeholders

◆ exercise the degree of care and skill of an experienced professional

◆ act with as much care, prudence and diligence in managing the company's affairs as when managing their personal affairs

◆ avoid actual and potential conflicts of interest and duty

◆ ensure the company complies with its legal obligations, these include not only such matters as submitting an annual report to government departments, but also Health and Safety and environmental issues. There has been a move in recent years to seek to hold a company and its directors responsible for accidents where there has been 'criminal intent'. There has been at least one case in the UK where a director was convicted of manslaughter.

◆ disclose all personal interests in contracts with the company.

Taking risks

This talk of 'care' and 'prudence' may give the wrong impression. It does not mean that the Board of a company cannot take risks. The Board will have to make decisions involving risks in order to achieve the company's objectives. Success should be the reward for risk. Taking a carefully evaluated risk does not guarantee success, nor does avoiding all forms of risk! Directors should not fear failure. The Board must identify opportunities and evaluate them, noting the benefits and risks involved, then make a decision on whether to go ahead. All the analysis in the world will not prevent a project failing or guarantee success.

Measuring performance

There is no doubt that there is government and public pressure in virtually every country for Boards to perform or improve performance; just what 'performance' means is not defined. The current measures of improved performance are based on 'added value' and in particular an improvement in the share price of the company. Earnings Per Share or EPS – i.e. profit per share – is a measure commonly used.

The Board will have its own definition of what it is seeking to achieve, whether to increase market share or increase dividends (99 per cent of the time these objectives will be exclusive). This 'strategy' should be made clear to shareholders. The shareholders and the Board of Directors will then have a common view of success and what 'performance' is.

In these circumstances being an effective director is not an easy job. It requires a professional focus and care. It is an important job; the prosperity of people and the nation depend on having successful directors.

The qualities of the ideal director

Many publications list the qualities of the ideal director. Sadly, perfection does not exist. There is more detail on page 40. A director must try to develop the 'ideal' qualities and continually seek to improve directorship skills. A potential director must not be deterred from joining a Board just because they do not match up to a list of ideal characteristics.

BOARD SUB-COMMITTEES

To help the working of the Board and spread the workload, the

Board of Directors is authorised to set up **Board sub-committees**. The usual sub-committees are, **Remuneration, Nomination** and **Audit**, but other special committees may be needed. It is not unusual for a bank to have a sub-committee responsible for monitoring **Financial Risk Management** or its **Assets and Liabilities**. The Board of a large processing group could well have a sub-committee responsible for **Environmental Matters and Issues**. This trend is becoming established and many companies include an Environmental Report in the report to shareholders.

Each sub-committee needs clear terms of reference, stating its objectives, composition and procedure for reporting to the Board. The objectives may be laid down in company law or in a stock exchange's Listing Rules, if the company's shares are quoted on a stock exchange, or simply decided by the Board to meet the needs of the company.

In summary, the common objectives of some sub-committees will be as follows.

Remuneration Committee

◆ Recommend the remuneration package for executive directors.

◆ Ensure that the process for setting remuneration for all staff is fair, unbiased, transparent and to seek to maintain equity between various categories of staff (not easy when groups of staff may be represented by different organisations).

◆ ensure remuneration offered by the Company is in line with the market and responsibilities.

> Some years ago a major public company reviewed the remuneration package for its chairman. The objective was to ensure it was fair in comparison with chairs of similar companies in Europe. In Europe the chairman's renumeration package frequently included benefits not usual in the UK, e.g. the free use of a holiday house. The Remuneration Committee put a value on these extra benefits and recommended a new package for the chairman. The package was put to the shareholders for approval. There was a storm of protest from shareholders. The package was seen as being far too generous and was rejected.

The storm continues. What is 'fair' and what 'excessive' has still to be defined. It could be that the storm would abate if shareholders approved the pay for all directors. A shareholder vote is recommended in some countries, while in others it is not the practice.

Membership of this sub-committee in a large company can be very interesting.

Nomination Committee

◆ Recommend in detail the size and composition of the Board.

◆ Locate suitable candidates to join the Board.

◆ Achieve the balance of skills and experience the company needs for its current and planned operations.

◆ Be responsible for advising directors on their continuing formal education on directorship, co-ordinated with education on the company's operations.

Nomination Committees are less common in the UK than in other countries and the Remuneration Committee often covers the responsibilities.

Audit Committee

- Oversee, review and enhance the company's external reporting procedures.

- Oversee the appointment and remuneration of the company's external auditors.

- Monitor the company's internal audit function.

- Monitor the accuracy and integrity of all financial statements.

- Monitor and enhance the company's internal financial reporting systems and controls.

- Ensure the company's reports internally and externally are to the highest industry standards.

The Audit Committee often has a very powerful role and frequently membership is subject to a great deal of scrutiny, particularly following a corporate collapse. One of the problems facing an Audit Committee is that it is reliant on what the company, its systems and executives tell it. Only in extreme circumstances would the Committee retain external advisors to prepare a separate report on any area of concern.

The needs of smaller companies

These Committees perform functions for larger companies that are handled in other ways by smaller companies.

◆ The function of the Remuneration Committee will, in a small company, probably be taken on by the non-executive director regularly collecting information about current pay packages for discussion with the other directors at a Board meeting. Even a company with one employee needs to ensure that the employee is paid fairly and in line with the market.

◆ A small company needs to think ahead; each person involved in the operation is important. The Nomination Committee may just take the form of a review, possibly once a year, of the retirement plans for each person. Illness of one person may indicate that thought needs to be given to how to replace the skills they have.

◆ The objectives of the Audit Committee may be dealt with by a non-executive director speaking to the company's auditor to establish that the company's accounting procedures are sound, accounting policies appropriate and results accurate. The director will report the result to the next Board meeting. If the company does not have its own internal audit function, the external auditors or another firm of professional accountants can fulfil the role.

There is not really any significant difference between the needs of a small and a large company; the difference is just one of scale.

WHO SHOULD BE ON A SUB-COMMITTEE?

Decisions are needed on who should be a member of the sub-committees. The members of the Audit Committee should all be non-executive because the objectives essentially include monitoring executive performance, whereas the Nominations Committee may have executive and non-executive directors because of the need for balance on the Board.

The discussions and recommendations of Board sub-committees must all be minuted. It is good practice for the minutes of sub-committee meetings to be circulated to all directors at least a week before the Board meeting and for the minutes to be reviewed and noted by the full Board.

Delegation of certain matters to Board sub-committees does not absolve the directors not on the sub-committees from their responsibilities as a director. To avoid difficulties it is good practice for Board sub-committees to make recommendations to the full Board, so all directors can participate in any final decision.

SUMMARY

◆ A company is a legal entity separate from its shareholders with a limited liability.

◆ Shareholders appoint directors to run the company.

◆ It is difficult to find a cast iron definition of a director's duties.

◆ All directors are equal.

◆ The title 'Director' must be used carefully.

◆ The Board can have sub-committees to help cover its responsibilities.

◆ A Board of Directors does not have a role separate from its Directors.

◆ The role and duties of a director and the Board are the same regardless of the size of the company, but they may be achieved in different ways.

$$\left(2\right)$$

The Role of a Director

Before anyone can decide whether to become a director, they need to know what is involved in 'directorship', what an individual needs to put into the company and what benefits will arise. This applies equally to employees joining their employer's Board, a non-executive director joining a Board or an entrepreneur becoming a director of a newly formed company.

Employees considering a Board appointment may believe that their knowledge of how the company works is all they need before becoming one of its directors. Experience has shown this is not true; the majority of company executives do not understand the role of a director. Everyone thinking about becoming a director should find out what is involved. Being a director is a job in its own right and must be done professionally.

THE DUTIES OF A DIRECTOR

The definition of what a director does is hedged around by negatives; sanctions, liabilities, conflicts, duties, responsibilities; a general lack of positive definition. This is the real life position in most countries. The vast majority of directors, however, do not experience any difficulty when acting as a director. It is a little like learning to drive. The early lessons discuss every potential danger, problem and responsibility and how to deal with them, but most drivers happily drive for years without a bump or scratch, let alone an accident.

The frequent, and often aggressively worded, public discussion of a director's duties and responsibilities may deter some from considering a directorship. It should not. The majority of directors do their job well and do it conscientiously. The public debate is actually helping to clarify a director's position and what is expected. Clarity always helps.

KEY POINT

The primary duty of a director is to act in good faith, making decisions in the best interests of the company. All else flows from this.

This basic duty to the company does not ignore the relationship with the shareholders, present and future. The shareholders expect and deserve a return on the investment they have made in the company.

Insolvency

If the company decides to cease trading or is forecast to become insolvent – i.e. will not able to pay its debts when they are due for payment – each director and the Board of Directors need to pay attention to protection of the company's creditors. The Board of Directors is expected to minimise creditors' losses. If it looks as if a company is heading for insolvency, the Board of Directors should take legal and financial advice on the best and most prudent courses of action. In most jurisdictions trading while insolvent is a criminal offence. Directors need to tread a very careful line when there is a chance the company may become insolvent or is insolvent and can no longer trade.

There is not a unified code of conduct for a director and it is unlikely there will ever be one in common law jurisdictions. The definition of a director's role will be found in various pieces of legislation and the recommendations and guidelines issued by professional bodies.

CONFLICT OF INTEREST

One issue that flows from the primary duty to act in good faith is that a director must be sensitive to conflicts of interest. A potential conflict of interest does not mean that an individual cannot join a Board. It does mean that a director must never be in a position where their involvement in another activity could influence their decision or comments at a Board meeting to the detriment of the company.

A director should even avoid the appearance of a conflict. It is good practice for a director to reveal to the Board of Directors all other interests they have, such as directorships in other companies, membership of government committees, even links with associations like the Boy Scouts!

An article in *The Economist* discussing the financial problems of Enron commented, '. . . several committee members faced financial conflicts of interest, generated only in part by Enron's donations to charities to which they were connected.'

Before joining a Board each director should register any potential conflict of interest. This can be done by preparing a written list to be noted by the Board at its meetings and recorded in the Minute Book. This is not a once and for all formality. The list needs to be kept up to date. A useful discipline is for each director to list all their interests each year. In New Zealand it is the practice to update the Register of Interests at each Board meeting.

Register of Interests

Some companies keep a **Register of Interests** listing the associations declared by each director. It can be very worthwhile declaring and recording the interests of a director's family members as well. Family interests become important when joining the Board of a company whose shares are quoted on a stock exchange, (**public company**). There are restrictions placed on share transactions by the directors and the families of directors by law and stock exchange regulations.

If a director becomes worried about a conflict of interest they should discuss the details with the company's chairman and if necessary with the company's lawyers; in serious cases the best course may be to decline the appointment or to resign.

A public company held a significant minority shareholding in two other public companies. One of the investor's executive directors joined the Boards of both investments as a non-executive director.

A trading dispute arose between the two investments. A Committee of Directors from the disputing parties was established to resolve it. The director nominated by the investor (a non-executive director of both of the disputing companies) chaired the committee. This director had to work in the best interest of three companies, the two in dispute and one investor: not at all easy.

This is the sort of conflict of interest that should be avoided if at all possible; perhaps an independent arbitrator would have been a better option.

Where a non-executive director also provides a service to the company, e.g. as a lawyer or an architect, they must not compromise their separate position as a director. The best course would be for the director to stop providing the service. If this is not practical, the director should pass the responsibility for providing the service to someone else in their firm and ensure that the firm has formal guidelines to ensure that the director and the person providing the service do not discuss company matters i.e. have a 'Chinese Wall'. In addition, the contract for the services should be reviewed and agreed by the Board. This is another circumstance where a director needs to take particular care.

STAKEHOLDERS – THE PROBLEM

A **stakeholder** is anyone with an interest in the prosperity of the company. Shareholders are clearly stakeholders; they have put their money into the company. But what of the company's employees? Many employees will have invested their energies, talent and years of their life in the company.

The Board of Directors guides the future of the company for the benefit of the shareholders. In practice, Boards also need to pay attention to the stakeholders who can have the power to influence the company, although legally, the Board is not responsible for the position of stakeholders.

The list of stakeholders includes:

◆ employees
◆ professional associations
◆ shareholders
◆ suppliers
◆ unions
◆ the general community (not a small group!).

All have an interest or 'stake' in the prosperity of the company. There is no doubt that a company is expected to act as a good citizen.

KEY POINT

The area of stakeholders and their relationship to the company and the Board is a very difficult one. It is developing and changing year by year.

In law, it is not the company's responsibility to take on any additional responsibility for these groups, nor do these groups have a legal call on the company. That said, directors cannot ignore stakeholders, particularly if the company faces some kind of crisis. A major chemical spillage or oil pollution, for example, can dramatically increase the range of stakeholders and interested parties who have an interest or claim on the attention of the company. In these circumstances the commercial credibility of the company may be jeopardised. The best interests of the company may require that the directors give attention and allocate resources to communicating with these groups.

Stakeholders can be volatile and with new technology, particularly the Internet, can pop up apparently from nowhere to become significant and powerful pressure groups.

> **A major oil company faced considerable opposition to its plans for disposing of two North Sea oil platforms. Consumers in Germany organised a boycott of the company's products. The result of this boycott was so serious that Board changed its decision. Once the change was made that particular pressure group melted away.**

It is worthwhile identifying the stakeholders who are influenced by and can influence the company. The process is called **stakeholder mapping**.

The people and organisations that could be considered as stakeholders in the merger of two large publicly quoted companies include:

ABC plc shareholders	Local Members of Parliament
XYZ plc shareholders	The European Union
Financial analysts	Mayors of towns where the companies have offices
Banks and institutional investors	Regulatory authorities
International media	UK regulators
ABC plc and XYZ plc staff and management	Joint Venture Partners
	Rating agencies

Stakeholders in smaller companies

A small company also has stakeholders, although they are likely to be fewer in number, generally in proportion to its local influence. If a local company proposes to relocate its factory to a 'green field site' 50 miles away the list of stakeholders would include:

- ◆ employees, current and to be recruited
- ◆ residents near the current and future locations
- ◆ local authorities in each location
- ◆ financing banks.

Society in general expects to have its interests and views taken into account by a company's Board when it is making decisions. At present, however, the law does not recognise these interests as considerations for the Board. The concept of stakeholders is emerging. The difficulty at present is, because stakeholders' interests can be so wide, the Board's responsibility is difficult to define.

THE JOB OF A DIRECTOR

A director's job cannot be easily defined. Anyone thinking of becoming a director should read the:

- ◆ international guidance produced by the Commonwealth Association for Corporate Governance

- ◆ *Guidelines for Directors* and *Standards for Directors* issued by the National Institute of Directors

- ◆ publications of professional organisations, e.g. Institute of Company Secretaries and Administrators, and leading accounting firms.

These will show the way. It is advisable to establish what local practice expects. Different countries have different laws and expectations of what a director needs to achieve and how they should go about it. In addition a director should see what the standards for directors are in other countries. Good directorship is a moveable feast and is being drawn towards the highest standards.

Non-executive directors

Non-executive and independent non-executive directors need the special ability, confidence and attitude of mind to be able to monitor the operations of the company and effectiveness of the company's management without becoming overly involved in detail. In essence this means monitoring the effectiveness of the executive directors, whom they will meet face to face at Board meetings.

Why are you there?

A potential director must be clear why they have been invited to join the Board. The reason may be that a current director plans to retire and the company needs to replace the experience or to add experience from another industry. The key words are '*the company needs*' the knowledge and experience. An appointment should not be made only to maintain the size and composition of the Board.

It may be that a person has the special skills or experience a company needs in its regular operations, or there could be a major development period during which a person's particular experience would help the Board's discussions.

Disqualification

Company law and a company's Articles of Association list circumstances in which a person may not be appointed as a director i.e. is 'disqualified'. An example is if the person is an undischarged bankrupt. The contents of the list vary between jurisdictions and it is worthwhile finding out just who is not qualified to be a director by the local laws.

THE QUALITIES AND ATTRIBUTES OF AN EFFECTIVE DIRECTOR

A Board of Directors is a group of individuals. Each director has their own personality; they are not expected to be clones. A director should be happy to work in this interactive environment. Working successfully on a Board requires certain qualities. A director is not expected to be mute; quite the contrary, they have joined the Board to make a contribution. The key point is to comment and question constructively.

An effective non-executive director on one Board was a professor at a major university, who never directly challenged anybody or openly criticised, but posed 'hypothetical questions' and made 'alternative assumptions'. Apart from these diplomatic skills, an important contribution he made to the company was the challenges to underlying assumptions others had taken as 'given'. At least one person on the Board needs to do this.

If you read the list of qualities or attributes recommended in the guidelines for directors issued by a professional institute, you will see those qualities a perfect director should have. But a director cannot be expected to have all of the desired attributes – even Superman is not perfect (try him with Kryptonite!). It is helpful, however, for a potential director to examine the list of desired qualities and talents. In summary the qualities often listed are:

AN EFFECTIVE DIRECTOR SHOULD POSSESS:

- sound business judgement
- integrity
- wide general knowledge
- breadth of vision
- an enquiring mind
- independence of thought
- the ability to work well in a team.

DO YOU HAVE TIME TO DO THE JOB PROPERLY?

When considering whether to become a director an individual must be prepared to commit to do whatever is necessary to perform the job professionally and allocate sufficient time to do the job well. The time requirement is not just the time attending Board meetings. It is necessary to study reports and recommendations (**Board papers**), as well as allocate time to learning about the company and the profession of being a 'director'. The New Zealand Institute of Directors estimates that a director should be prepared to allocate three days a month to each directorship. Reading, considering and responding to even a simple set of Board Papers can take many hours. Time is a commitment of every director, including executive directors.

For an executive director the commitment to a directorship may cut into current normal working hours. For a retired professional, it may mean time away from the garden. For a working professional, it will be time away from clients.

The commitment to time limits the number of directorships an individual can hold and still do a good job. There are only 24 hours in a day!

Multiple directorships

All countries are sensitive to the maximum number of active
directorships one person should have, but there is generally no
legislation. The Hong Kong Institute of Directors recommends 'a
reasonable number consistent with fulfilling fiduciary duties'. The
New Zealand Institute of Directors asks 'Do you have time to do the
job properly?'

Attendance at meetings

Some jurisdictions have clear ideas about the number of meetings a
director should attend. In Australia each company's Annual Report
to shareholders lists each individual directors' attendance at Board
and sub-committee meetings. The UK treats persistent non-
attendance as default and the model form of Articles of Association
requires a director to resign if they do not attend a Board meeting
during six months.

Seeing the big picture

The Board deals with shaping the future of the company. Directors
must be able to avoid the temptation to discuss and try to resolve
current problems to the exclusion of discussing the future and
developing strategy. This can be particularly hard for executive
directors who, by definition, spend the majority of their time
involved in running a particular part of an organisation. Day-to-day
problems should not be delegated upwards!

LEARNING ABOUT THE COMPANY

A potential director needs to understand the inter-relationship of
different parts of the business – sales, development, production,
finance, marketing, distribution – and be able to commit the time to
study how the company organisation works. To be able to find their
way round an organisation a director needs to 'do the knowledge'.

This is essential in order to be effective in the boardroom because each director needs a sufficient grasp of all the areas of the business to be able to ask sensible questions and understand the answers.

> At one successful company, the handover plans set up for a new executive director always included as the first stage meetings with the executive directors of each area of the business, before getting involved in the detail of the job being handed over.

KEY POINT

Knowledge will permit a director to challenge and evaluate the assumptions of others.

AN OPEN AND FRANK EXCHANGE OF VIEWS

A director must be happy and confident to take part in discussions openly and frankly regardless of differing views. It is easier to make good decisions if there has been an open debate rather than approving with a wise-looking nod and a quiet 'Yes'.

Boards make decisions that have long-term effects. A director must be confident to be part of a decision that will have a significant effect on the company. Each director should be able to be part of the process of taking a measured and controlled risk. No amount of information, research or analysis will entirely eliminate the risks from decisions and a director must be comfortable with being part of a decision that could go wrong.

It is sometimes difficult for an executive director to participate fully in all Board discussions, particularly when it involves an area controlled by a colleague. For example, will an engineering director be happy to discuss and challenge the chief financial officer on the objectives and risks of a financing strategy? If the answer is 'No' the engineering director really should not be on the Board. Hard, but realistic.

Each director cannot have the same level expertise in all subjects, but must have an appreciation of the basics and be sufficiently confident to ask questions. Non-executive directors can have a similar problem: do they have sufficient knowledge of the business to debate fully and confidently with executive directors?

> **The primary cause of the collapse of a major bank was the losses generated by one of the bank's derivatives traders, but a contributory factor was the Board's reluctance to challenge the underlying assumptions of the information presented and the system of control.**

DIRECTORS OF PRIVATE OR SMALL COMPANIES

There are special considerations if an individual is thinking about joining the Board of a private company or a small company. A **private** company is one whose shares are not traded on a stock exchange or by individuals. A **small** company is one where a small number of shareholders, perhaps only one person or the members of one family, nominate directors to the Board – i.e. ownership and direction are held within a small group of individuals, although the company's operations may be large.

Special care is needed if shareholders are also directors, as well as part of the management team. There is great potential for the definition of responsibilities and duties to become blurred. Research suggests that controlling shareholders tend to appoint family members as executive directors.

The law does not recognise a combined 'owner-director-manager' role or any merging of responsibilities, nor does good corporate governance. Any person acting in three roles should be extremely careful. At a shareholders' meeting act only as the owner of part of the business, at a Board meeting only as a director and as a manager when managing. Non-executive directors can help keep the roles separate by highlighting any overlap.

If care is not taken it will be unclear whether a meeting is a shareholders' meeting, a Board meeting, an operating budget meeting or a family lunch!

THE PROS AND CONS OF BEING A DIRECTOR

Your liabilities as a director

The shareholders do not directly own the assets of the company. The management of the company's assets and the future of the company is delegated to the directors; therefore, not unreasonably, the shareholders expect directors to stand behind their decisions. A consequence of this is that the liability of a director is unlimited against claims by the shareholders or the government for wrongful acts. A claim will only succeed if there has been wrongdoing, and most people are honest.

It is unusual for a director to face a claim from shareholders for compensation or to face criminal proceedings, despite the growing trend of holding directors publicly responsible for the results of their decisions.

Limits on remuneration

A predictable response from a director will be that directors should be paid adequately for the responsibility they bear and the cost of insurance.

> I recently read a magazine article proposing that members of the Board's Remuneration Committee should be responsible for any 'excessive' salary, bonus or share options granted to executive directors.

So far there is no definition of what 'excessive' means. In the USA it has been suggested that within a company the highest paid employee should not receive more than 25 times the amount earned by the lowest paid. Directors will have to see how and whether this idea develops.

Liability and indemnity insurance

To avoid discouraging skilled and experienced people from becoming directors and joining a Board, an insurance policy has been developed: Directors and Officers Liability and Indemnity Insurance. The attitude towards this type of insurance differs between jurisdictions. In some countries many directors take out such an insurance policy; in others it is not popular. In some countries the terms of the insurance must be agreed and the premium paid by the individual director. In others there is a company policy which all directors can join with the premium paid by the company. In yet other areas there is a standard policy and the cost is shared between the director and the company.

Other risks
In addition to possible legal exposures, a potential director must think of 'reputation risk' – i.e. whether they wish to become associated with a particular business. Some people may not want to become a director of a company involved in tobacco or meat processing or with significant manufacturing operations in less developed countries where conditions of employment are poor.

There is also the chance, somewhat remote, of being accused of wrong doing or being associated with others accused. All these risks need to be thought over.

The benefits
Much of what we have written deals with potential liabilities, downsides and the risks of being a director; what are the benefits?

Remuneration package
Before deciding to become a director or joining a Board an individual should have a clear idea of how much their skill, experience and effort should be worth. Whether a company will agree to pay the 'worth' is another matter. Details of the remuneration package for a director will vary with the local culture and economy and may include some or all of:

◆ fees
◆ pension
◆ share options
◆ reimbursement of expenses
◆ office/clerical support for work on company business.

There is a very interesting debate about whether all directors should own shares in the company. There is no recommended course. The Articles of Association of some companies require a director to own a minimum number of shares, **qualifying shares**.

Those in favour of directors owning shares argue that it unifies the thinking of the shareholders and the Board, as well as providing an incentive to increase the value of the company. Those against argue that non-executive and independent non-executive directors need to take an independent view of all decisions and concentrate on achieving long-term goals rather than short-term share price gains. Some managers would like non-executive directors to be paid in shares or share options, because at present under most accounting practices, there would be no cost to the company.

> I have the view that directors should buy shares in the company, but the object of this book is to make potential directors aware of the issues involved in directorship, not to argue a particular position.

Specific guidance on directors' pay can usually be obtained from one of the 'reward surveys' published by recruitment companies or university departments or similar institutions.

Some directors will be surprised to learn that in many jurisdictions a director is not automatically entitled to any fee or even reimbursement of expenses – a very strange situation considering the important role the director plays in a company and economy.

Before deciding to become a director, you should have a clear idea of what level of remuneration would be appropriate for your circumstances.

♦ A professional providing services to a number of companies will want to ensure that the remuneration is adequate and compensates for the effort and time taken away from other earning activities.

♦ Someone who has retired from full-time work will want adequate remuneration for the time taken away from other activities.

♦ An executive with an income from the company through a service contract may expect something extra to recognise the added responsibilities.

KEY POINT

Generally an executive director does not benefit from appointment as a director. Any directors' fees are waived and any fees earned from membership of the Board of another company will be paid to the employer.

There have been studies into the relationship between profit sharing and performance that conclude there is a positive link with company performance only where the profit shared is closely related to recent profit performance.

Clearly there are ways to balance fees and/or shares in a remuneration package. This is an issue for an intending director to investigate during the review meeting after the due diligence process (see page 72, Chapter 3). Any requirement to own shares means that personal money is at risk.

There are also differences of opinion on whether each director should have the same remuneration structure or one tailored to individual preferences. Directors' remuneration in large companies is likely to be fairly standard and already approved by shareholders, hence difficult to change. In a smaller organisation it may be possible for the package to be negotiated individually with the chairman. There may be a standard package for each director, with room to adjust the package to suit an individual's preferences.

Institutes of directors generally recommend that the 'pot' of directors' fees should in principle be shared equally, with extra only paid for extra work, e.g. time on Board sub-committees.

The value of the package for the director must be sufficient to attract people with the skills and experience the company wants and be commensurate with the time, effort and liabilities of directors. If this is not the case, few of the right people will come forward to serve. A useful comparison for the package is with the hourly or daily fees charged by other professionals, e.g. lawyers or accountants. This information can usually be found in professional surveys.

Non-financial benefits
Are there any other benefits to a directorship, apart from the money? It is for each individual to give their own answer.

A director plays a vital role in the development of a company, hence influences the prosperity of all stakeholders and the national economy. Many directors are motivated by job satisfaction from making a contribution to a company and adding value to its operation. Experienced people and those with business skills really can make a positive difference to the way a company develops, particularly in small and newly established companies. They can make a difference to company performance. Taking a 'non-executive' view of what is going on can be every bit as useful as running the business day by day.

> The Board of a small company involved in a cyclical business got a great deal of help from a non-executive director who was cautious and questioning when the executives were optimistic, but optimistic and encouraging when the executives were cautious and depressed. The company grew steadily into a major profit earner.

If a person wishes to become a professional director, accumulating a portfolio of directorships will provide an income base. Each directorship will add to personal skills and business knowledge as well as increasing the network of contacts.

There is also a certain amount of prestige in being a director and influencing the course of a company, despite the hard work.

The intangible benefits of being a director should not be underrated. Success always brings a sense of satisfaction and pleasure. Aggregate company prosperity has a big influence on the prosperity of the whole economy, and a director plays an important role in that prosperity.

Finding a directorship
If having weighed the pros and cons you decide to go ahead and become a director there is not a clear way of finding the right

position if you have not already been offered one. Some professional organisations provide the service of suggesting names of potential directors to companies. The organisation is retained by a company to find a suitable director. Those who want to be a non-executive director will find that most frequently positions are gained by personal invitation. Exactly the best way for an individual to get an invitation to join the Board of their employer is best left to the individual to decide!

There is not a season for appointing a new director to the board. In practical terms a director can join a Board at any time.

SUMMARY

- The primary duty of a director is to act in good faith, making decisions in the best interests of the company.

- The role of a director is often not well defined.

- There are guidelines and standards for directors that help understand what is needed.

- A director must allocate enough time to do the job well.

- The law tends to impose liabilities and responsibilities.

- Directors and Officers Liability and Indemnity Insurance exists to help.

- Directors should be paid for their work in line with other professionals.

- There are benefits other than just financial ones.

3

Finding Out About the Company

DUE DILIGENCE

Before joining the board of a company a potential director needs to know how the company is organised, what its operations are, what the company has achieved and where it is going. This process of familiarisation is called **due diligence** and must be completed before the final decision is made whether or not to join a Board.

There are a few absolutely basic questions to be answered:

- What does the company do?
- How does it do it?
- What has the company achieved?
- What does the company want to achieve?

The answers to these questions will help provide the answers to the key questions for the individual:

- Can I, as a director, help the company achieve its objectives?

- Do I have the skills or knowledge that will be useful to the company and help improve its operations?

Directors are not appointed to make up numbers, but to help a company achieve its strategic objectives. The Board can be thought of as an organisational tool that sets, and helps to achieve, a company's strategy.

The Institute of Chartered Secretaries and Administrators in the UK has produced guidelines discussing the due diligence process.

A potential director needs to understand:

- the regulations surrounding the company
- how the company operates
- how the company is organised and administrated
- the company's recent and current financial position
- the company's long-term goals
- what progress has been made towards achieving the long-term goals.

The sequence of events up to the formal appointment to the Board of Directors should be tailored to the way the company operates and to local practice.

Some part of the information-gathering included here as part of due diligence – e.g. visits to locations – may be deferred until after the director has been appointed and will be continued as part of the director's **induction**.

The Commonwealth Association for Corporate Governance recommends that the process should take the following form:

1. The potential director carries out the due diligence process.

2. The potential director receives and accepts an offer to join the Board of Directors.

3. Induction of the new director is completed.

4. The new director is formally appointed to the Board of Directors and the full responsibilities and liabilities of directorship start.

Whatever the sequence of steps, sufficient information must be available for a potential director to understand the company and answer the key questions.

Some of the information a potential director will see during the due diligence process will be highly confidential. It is not unusual for a company to request a potential director to sign a **confidentiality agreement** or give a verbal undertaking that they will not discuss or reveal any of the information seen. The Board of Directors is at the very centre of a company's strategy and the company could be damaged if any information seen during due diligence is passed on to others formally or informally, deliberately or accidentally – for example, at a social gathering.

There may be some pieces of information that are so sensitive that the full detail will not be revealed until a director joins the Board. This is quite understandable and acceptable provided that sufficient information is given to enable a potential director to fully understand the company.

WHAT HAPPENS IN THE DUE DILIGENCE PROCESS

The process starts with the essential step of understanding the basics of the company and its operations.

The documents to be seen first are the company's Memorandum and Articles of Association.

The Memorandum of Association details all the activities the company is authorised to undertake. The company's current operations will form part of the list, but there will probably be many more activities the company could do if the Board so wished.

Ultra vires

A potential director needs to understand the concept of **ultra vires** – i.e. acting beyond authority and how it is applied in the country where the company is registered. Ultra vires can apply in both the narrow sense of a company carrying out an activity not authorised in its Memorandum of Association and in the wider sense of entering into a gratuitous transaction. In addition there is the possibility of a Board acting ultra vires. The concept is important, but complex. The company secretary or the company's lawyer will be able to explain in detail.

The principal of ultra vires has been abolished or modified by legislation in some jurisdictions, in others it is still covered by common law. In 1997 in Hong Kong an Amendment Ordinance abolished the concept of the ultra vires rule for companies; a company now has the capacity and rights, powers and privileges of an individual person. The position is similar in New Zealand. In Australia the concept of ultra vires still applies to companies. There is little point in discussing this technical matter in detail here except to say that a potential director should find out what the current position is in their country.

Memorandum and Articles of Association

The Articles of Association detail the internal rules of the company such as:

◆ minimum and maximum number of directors that can be appointed to the Board

◆ minimum number of Board meetings each year

◆ the quorum for a Board meeting

- number of votes required to pass a resolution at a Board meeting

- when meetings of shareholders are needed

- how shareholder meetings should be run

- items to be on the agenda for the Annual General Meeting of shareholders

- the period of notice required of the place and date of directors and shareholders meetings

- who is disqualified from being a director

- whether directors should own shares before appointment

- how and when share certificates are to be issued

- how the chairman is appointed.

Many companies have a copy of the Memorandum and Articles of Association available on the table at all Board meetings.

Company law and the Articles of Association attempt to control the relationship between the director and the company. This tends to be done in a negative way by listing what cannot be done, e.g. restricting share transactions between the company and its directors and perhaps the directors' families.

Statement of Board Reserved Powers

There is often a useful attempt to define the decisions and responsibilities of the Board. These will be found in a **Statement of Board Reserved Powers** – a list of all the powers the Board keeps for itself. A typical example might include:

◆ Recommendation on the remuneration of auditors.

◆ Recommendation to change auditors.

◆ Approval of the auditors' engagement letter and Audit Scope Memorandum.

◆ Review of the auditors' recommendations and observations.

◆ Approval of all circulars and other documents, including those required by any stock exchange, to be sent to shareholders.

◆ Approval of press releases on matters decided by the Board.

◆ Approval of Interim and Final Accounts and Reports.

◆ Approval of Interim Dividends and recommendation of a Final Dividend.

◆ Approval of all significant changes in accounting policies and practices.

◆ Approval of all changes to the organisation of senior management.

◆ Approval of individual items of capital expenditure in excess of a stated amount.

This is just an illustration to show the type of matters the Board might want to be involved in.

In a joint venture company very often there is a long debate about what authority and powers the Board will exercise and what will be allocated to the management team. This is an important issue, partly because companies have different approaches and systems, but also because such clarity means that the Board and management team can build trust between them.

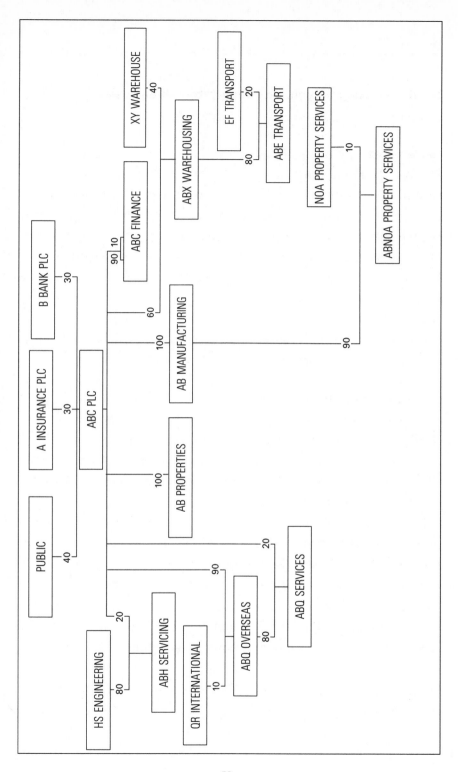

A potential director will be interested to see the Board's work plan for the year. This is discussed on page 132.

Paperwork

Much of this book has described the duties, responsibilities and liabilities of a director, which are considerable. It will therefore be no surprise to learn that upon becoming a director there are forms to be completed. The company secretary will guide a new director through the formalities; there will be returns for the Registrar of Companies, for the company itself and for the stock exchange, if the company's shares are quoted.

The company secretary should be expert in these areas and what is needed, but all directors must be aware of them as well.

COMPANY STRUCTURE

After studying the company's legal framework, the potential director needs to get to grips with the business or businesses the company operates. This involves examining a list of the companies and locations involved in the operations and details of how they are organised. Some companies perform one function, e.g. manufacturing widgets, while others become involved in other parts of the business or other businesses, e.g. storage, distribution or other activities. The company structure can range from one company owned by two shareholders to a complex 'wiring diagram'.

In this example, B Bank plc's shareholdings in both ABC plc and ABC Finance produces the potential for a conflict of interests.

Supporting the diagram should be a description of the function of each company, where it is registered and located, together with an outline of its operation and the number of staff employed at each location. At a later date, after joining the board and seeing the results of each operation, it is advisable for a new director to visit, at the least, the most important operating locations to see the physical features, sense the atmosphere and meet key managers.

A useful question to ask when visiting a location is, 'What is the most difficult problem in doing your job?'

During a due diligence visit to a direct mailing company the post room manager was asked this and replied 'Balancing the daily postage account at the Post Office'. Further probing revealed that there was a large amount unpaid, for which the company did not have a record. An interesting reflection on the system of control.

The Board of Directors cannot work in a vacuum and must be, and be seen to be, part of a company's operation. Corporate ivory towers are obsolete and need to be demolished to make room for open discussion!

With the answer to the question, 'What does the Company do?' a potential director should establish how the company is organised. The answer will be found in some form of organisation chart showing the layers of management and the main responsibilities for each major area with a brief curriculum vitae for all directors and senior managers.

The part of the chart dealing with the Board should include details of all Board sub-committees, their composition and terms of reference.

Although a director is unlikely to need to contact the company's main advisors, it is useful to know the name of the firms providing legal advice, the auditors and the company's main bankers, if only to ensure that there is no chance of a conflict of interest. Directors need this information; they do have the right to take external advice at the company's expense.

PERFORMANCE

The next item on a potential director's agenda is to look at the company's past results, i.e. financial and operating performance, what the company plans to achieve and what the strategy is. All of this information should have been discussed and agreed at earlier meetings of the Board, hence will be recorded and filed in the company's Minute Book.

The chart for a large company might look like that shown opposite:

Financial results

It should be sufficient to review just the last three years of financial results (the company's Statutory Accounts, discussed on page 103). The Statutory Accounts will mention any outstanding disputes or litigation. Regardless of any note in the accounts, it is worthwhile asking for a list of outstanding disputes and an assessment of the likely outcome.

Operating results

Equally important is to review the operating results for the same period. These provide more detailed information of how the

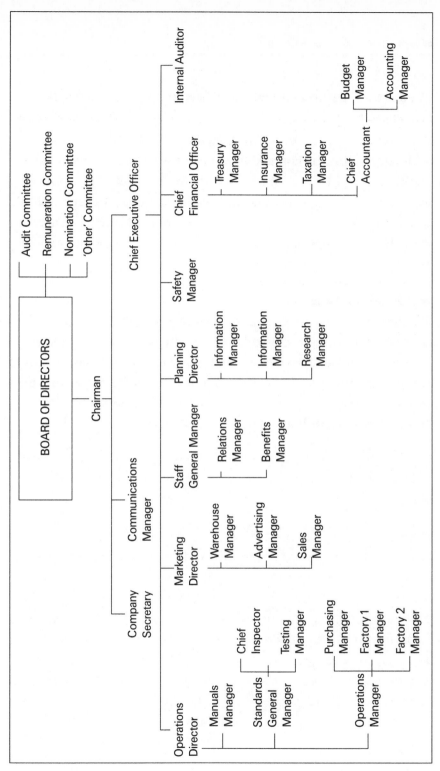

company has performed against its short term targets (often called a **budget**) and will also include the results of surveys of customers and staff. Taken together they give a picture of what the company has achieved and how it has performed against agreed targets.

The Board will have received and approved short-term forecasts; a review of these will give a potential director an idea of what tasks lie ahead for the organisation.

Strategy Paper and Business Plan

In addition to these reports the latest Strategy Paper and the Business Plan should be studied, thus bringing together the company's strategy and tactics. The Strategy Paper and Business Plan should include a section on each key area of the business. It is tempting to focus on the company's financial side, but a company will not be successful if it does not have a plan for such areas as 'information technology' and 'people' ('human resources').

It will be worrying if the company's strategy document is not clearly written. It is the blueprint for the future of the company and it is not possible to achieve goals that are only perceived through a mist.

Comparison with competitors

With luck there will also be a report and analysis of the performance of competitors in the same industry and a comparison with the company's own results. This adds an important external comparison of the company's operating performance, e.g. units produced, units sold, units in stock, in addition to the measurement against the company's own targets. There have been recommendations in many studies emphasising the importance of comparing performance with competitors and watching what is happening in the industry.

Operating reports are often too inward looking. In the UK, the Department of Trade and Industry runs a series of useful benchmarking surveys.

Bringing it all together

The financial reports are important, of that there can be no doubt, but total money numbers by themselves don't tell the full story, nor do purely operating figures. The financial figures need to be linked to what is happening in the company and its operations. Operating results need to include money numbers. If a company uses only operating targets, in the short term the results may look impressive, but the company may have serious fundamental problems.

> A due diligence visit to a factory showed that there were piles of finished and semi-finished items. Inquiry revealed that the production accounting system was driven by 'machine utilisation' and the factory was encouraged to keep high stock levels so that sales could be met quickly. In buoyant trading this approach seemed to work, but with a high finance cost. When demand dropped there were substantial unsaleable goods.

Customer surveys

Particular attention should be paid to reports on the reaction of customers and potential customers to the company's products and services. Surveys of customers and potential customers are often long and not always easy to understand. Help may be needed to understand the conclusions and an explanation from the chairman or marketing director will help. This is vital information for every new director, whether executive or non-executive. In some companies the Board commissions its own customer satisfaction survey.

Minute Book

The Minute Book will include the record of past meetings of the Board and its decisions. The minutes for the last three years will provide excellent background on the important discussions and action. Reports from Board sub-committees will be part of the minutes; these should be read as well.

Staff reports

The reports to the Board should include some report on staff and their morale. In a large company this may be a survey indicating whether staff understand the company's goals and what their attitude to the company is. On a smaller scale the report may be a summary of the reasons given for resigning and the periodic meetings with staff. A useful regular report is a graph showing staff turnover (number of staff leaving the company compared to the number of staff employed) compared to the average for the industry. This area is discussed further on page 88.

RISK MANAGEMENT

The management of the risks facing a company has always been the responsibility of the Board, but it should be an item on the Board's agenda. A risk is any happening that will damage the company or prevent it achieving its goals. It is not possible to eliminate risk; all that can be done is to minimise and manage the effects on the company.

The responsibility for dealing with the detail of the risk management process may be given to an existing Board sub-committee, such as the Audit Committee, or a separate Risk Committee. In some cases the Board itself will deal with the detail.

A potential director should review the following areas:

◆ Identification of types of risks, e.g. financial risk, the effects of changes in interest rates, etc. or business risk, factory accidents, etc.

◆ Analysis of each risk, detailing the likelihood of the risk happening and the possible loss to the company.

◆ Ways to handle the risk to minimise the effects on the company.

◆ Establishment of preferred ways to manage the effect and implementing and testing them.

◆ Regular reporting of progress and results to the Board.

◆ Board reviews, discussion and action on the reports.

In the company's Minute Book there should be copies of the regular reports to the Board on:

◆ important incidents

◆ risk management plans adopted/tested with results

◆ result of Internal Audit reviews of internal controls and systems

◆ current financial exposures and value of any derivatives

◆ the Treasury Department's plan for the next period.

WHAT HAS THE DUE DILIGENCE PROCESS PRODUCED SO FAR?

At this point the key questions will have been answered:

- ◆ What does the company do?
- ◆ How does it do it?
- ◆ What does the company seek to achieve?
- ◆ What has been achieved so far?
- ◆ What is still to be done?
- ◆ What has the company done to manage the risks it faces?

REGULATIONS

There may be special regulations or laws governing the company.

Listing Rules

If the company's shares are listed on a stock exchange, the company will be subject to the stock exchange's **Listing Rules**. A potential director should understand these regulations. This is an important area for all directors. The Listing Rules will deal with such matters as:

- ◆ reports needed if it is proposed to buy another company

- ◆ when public announcements should be made, e.g. changes in capital structure, major assets purchases, changes in the officers of the company, particularly independent non-executive directors.

The Listing Rules also deal with procedural matters defining the Stock Exchange's requirements for different sizes or types of transaction. This summary, from The Stock Exchange of Hong Kong Limited, issued in July 1995, is a good example of the range of requirements.

Req/Type	Notify Exchange	Press Advert	Circular to Shareholders	Shareholder Approval	Accountants Report
Substantial	Yes	Yes	Yes	Yes	Yes
Major	Yes	Yes	Yes	Yes	Yes
Discloseable	Yes	Yes	Yes	No	No
Share	Yes	Yes	No	No	No

These may well have changed and the requirements will differ
between stock exchanges, but the summary remains a useful
example.

If a director accepts appointment to the Board of a company whose
shares are quoted on a stock exchange, it will probably be required
that a newspaper announcement of the appointment be made within
a certain time.

Environmental regulations

The company's operations may be highly regulated because of the
potential effect on the environment. Any special regulations should
be studied. Certain industries, e.g. plastic foam manufacturers, are
subject to very specific safety regulations. In the UK, the Health and
Safety regulations are very comprehensive.

Boards may think there is not any exposure to environmental risk,
but this is not always the case.

In the UK, a truck driver tipped a load of a relatively inert
chemical into the wrong hopper, causing significant pollution
to the local water supply.

In Switzerland, a tanker driver wrongly tipped a load into the Rhine causing massive pollution to the river.

Both companies were sued for substantial compensation.

Other regulations

The company's business may involve operating a franchise. If so, the essential requirements of the franchise agreement must be reviewed.

There may be legal limits on what a company can do. A vintner commented that in the UK it is illegal for a wine producer to operate a distillery on the same site. Any restriction should be noted.

There could also be specific legislation governing the company's operations, for example as a 'corporate service provider' or a provider of trust services in the Isle of Man. Consideration of these special requirements will lead a potential director to ask to see the regulations. Directors need to know and understand the framework in which the company operates.

There is clearly much to do. A director's job is special and the responsibilities are wide; they are not to be taken lightly.

HELP WITH DUE DILIGENCE

There are a number of people who will help a potential director through the due diligence process. The chairman, company secretary, chief financial officer, other directors, the company's auditors and lawyers will all help.

The chairman is responsible for ensuring that all the information a potential director needs is made available and that people are free to give explanations and advice. The company secretary will probably make all the arrangements.

There are many ways to complete the process of learning about the company. The easiest and probably best place to start is with the company secretary, to review the records of the meetings of the Board and its committees together with the company's documents.

The company secretary will have a copy of the company's Memorandum and Articles of Association and will be able to answer questions on how each article operates. In addition the company secretary will have copies of the company's Reports to Shareholders (annual and perhaps quarter- and/or semi-annual) describing the operations of the company, and listing the operating locations and the financial results. This will be a good start.

The Minute Book held by the company secretary will provide much useful information and history to a potential director. It is likely that a potential director will wish to discuss the company's past and forecast financial results with the chief financial officer and may also seek clarification of the company's accounting policies. Reviewing the minutes of recent Audit Committee meetings will highlight whether there have been any difficulties in producing the accounts for shareholders.

The chairman should arrange production of the other information needed. Any queries a potential director may have on any document, or any lack of information, should be initially directed to the chairman, the 'boss' of the Board. Discretion on whether to answer questions directly or to arrange for another to answer rests with the chairman. If pieces of information do not exist or have not been made available, the reasons should be discussed with the chairman.

> When doing due diligence I noticed that the documents did not include a Forecast Balance Sheet, because the company did not produce one. At an interview with the chairman it was agreed that the Board would discuss the benefits of having a forecast financial position at its next meeting.

REVIEW MEETING

When the due diligence process is complete there should be a meeting between the potential director and the chairman to ensure that all matters are clear.

It is at this meeting that, most probably, the potential director will be asked when they will be able decide whether or not they will join the Board. Before making a decision the potential director must be confident that they have a good understanding of the company, what it plans to achieve and are also comfortable working with the other directors and the senior management team.

If the due diligence process has been completed successfully, before deciding to join the Board, the potential director should clarify some personal matters.

It is important that the chairman makes clear:

- what particular contribution the Board expects from the new director

- what the director's remuneration will be

- how long the appointment could be for

- whether the director is expected to own shares in the company

- whether there is a share option scheme for directors

- the position on Directors Liability and Indemnity Insurance. The regulations on this type of insurance vary from country to country where insurance cover is available. It may be that the company can pay the premium or the director may have to pay all or part of the premium themselves.

There is another personal aspect of due diligence – whether the potential director should be paid for the time spent on the process, even if the final outcome is that the potential director does not join the Board. It seems only fair that there should be some payment for the time spent. The process, if done correctly, will take quite a few hours even for a small company; in the case of a complex company, a day or so.

If the decision is to join the Board, it is the responsibility of the new director to get right up to speed on current problems facing the company so that they start contributing at meetings quickly.

Due diligence is a process for all potential directors
The due diligence process described is aimed at all potential directors. A company executive considering an appointment to the Board for the first time may believe they know everything about the company and do not need to go through the due diligence process.

This is not true; a newly appointed marketing director needs just as much background information on the company's strategy, results, product and organisation as a new non-executive director; the process is the same.

In joint venture companies or subsidiaries a director may be nominated to the Board by the major shareholder. Even in these circumstances, the nominated director must complete the due diligence process, so they can carry out their responsibilities fully.

Appointment of a new director

Directors are actually appointed by the shareholders, but the company's Articles of Association will usually allow directors to be appointed during the year. The process of appointment can be for the new director to be appointed to the Board and at the next Annual General Meeting, resign and seek re-election. Alternatively they are nominated and elected to the Board at the next Annual General Meeting.

The Board should operate as a team. At some stage before attending the first Board meeting a new director should meet all the other directors individually. Probably the best time to do this is after having accepted the offer to join the Board, but before formal appointment.

SUMMARY

After reading all the documents and hearing all the explanations you should understand:

◆ how the company/group is organised and who owns whom

- the extent to which ultra vires applies to the company

- what exclusive powers the Board has and what its responsibilities are

- the company's long-term goals and how the company has performed against its own targets, long-term plans and competitors

- the need for the Board to monitor current operations and hold management accountable

- the company's customers' attitude to the company's products and services and the opinions of those who are not customers

- the staff's attitude towards the company

- the Board's and directors' legal obligations

- the laws and regulations framework within which the company operates

- what information you need to register, if you become a director

- what contribution is expected of you

- what remuneration you will receive

- how well the individuals on the Board work together and whether you can work well with them?

You should now be able to answer the important questions mentioned at the beginning of this chapter:

- Can I, as a director, help the company achieve its objectives?

♦ Do I have the skills or knowledge that will be useful to the company and will add to its operation?

The decision is now yours.

CHECKLIST

Has the Board:

☐ defined the powers and authority of the Board and of management

☐ produced a clear statement of the company's long-term goals

☐ identified the resources needed to achieve the long-term goals and taken action to ensure these are available

☐ actively monitored current operations

☐ held management accountable for the actual financial and operating results compared to targets, long-term goals and the results of competitors

☐ considered the views and needs of shareholders, customers, staff and other stakeholders when making decisions

☐ considered the work and recommendations of sub-committees and taken action

☐ reviewed the remuneration of senior management

☐ produced policies (courses of action) and strategies (long-term plans of action) for major parts of the business:
  – finance
  – people
  – risk management
  – environment
  – compliance with regulations
  – customer and products

☐ regularly received, debated and made decisions on reports covering:
  – customers' attitude to product and services
  – competitors' strengths
  – staff attitude to the company, understanding of long-term goals, whether they have the resources needed to achieve the goals
  – current and future financing for the company
  – managing the adverse effects of changes in financial markets
  – managing the adverse effects of business risks facing the company

☐ worked to an annual plan of work

☐ met its legal obligations in good time

☐ kept clear records of its meetings?

4

Information Directors Need Before a Board Meeting

Directors are charged with monitoring the company's current performance and securing its future. The responsibilities are usually summarised as:

◆ to set objectives (strategy), together with intermediate targets
◆ to monitor performance against agreed targets.

AGENDA

An agenda will be sent to directors before each Board meeting listing the items to be discussed at the meeting. The Chairman will be responsible for approving the items on the agenda, although it will probably be drafted by the CEO and the Company Secretary. The agenda items will be comprised of items in the Board's work plan (see page 132), action items from previous meetings and new issues (see page 95).

THE IMPORTANCE OF GOOD INFORMATION

The Board will only be able to set goals and monitor performance if its members are well informed. All directors need to ensure they have all the information they need to do their job. in most cases, the company will provide the required information, but if not, the company is responsible for helping a director get it from other sources.

A quotation from Sun Tsu: 'Anyone who is to start military operations in one part of the country should know the condition of the country as a whole . . . knowing the situation goes on not only before, but also after the formation of plans. . .'

Good and relevant information is absolutely essential. Directors must arrive at Board meetings well briefed and fully armed to take part in discussions and decision making. In practice this may be difficult because information is not always available in good time and can be incomplete. The Board, led by the chairman, needs to ensure it gets clear Board papers in good time; the management is responsible for meeting directors' needs.

BACKGROUND INFORMATION

It is not sufficient for a director simply to have a report on the company's current operations; a wider range of information is needed. The company operates in an industry and in a regional and national economy. It may operate in many parts of the world. The external influences on an industry and from economic trends will affect the company's current operation and ability to meet long-term goals. Directors need to know what is going on around them and the company.

The industry

There is very little which remains unchanged in this world. There may be significant real or forecast changes in the industry, e.g. new technology, new methods of distribution or regrouping of companies. The Board should have a view on major changes, either to adopt them, if it looks as if the company will benefit, or to ignore them, if the Board is not convinced that the change will produce a return. Not all changes work – not all change is for the better – but directors need to know what is going on in the industry.

Executive directors will probably have the best idea of what is happening in the industry, but non-executive directors must also have a view, not an opinion filtered by the executive directors.

Closed group thinking, where collectively a group of individuals finds it difficult to accept an idea that conflicts with current thinking, can affect every organisation.

Several large American companies rejected Edison's idea for a light bulb because: 'it will never work'. The quartz watch was first developed in Switzerland, but not accepted by the local industry. Japanese companies proved its worth.

Probably the easiest way to get industry information is for the company to arrange for each director to receive a copy of industry magazines or newspapers. This is a cheap and effective way for all to stay up to speed with current thinking.

The economy

Trends in the national and world economy will affect a company in some way.

First, a director should understand what particular elements of the economy could affect the company generally and then which may affect the company specifically.

In a consumer-led business, increases in interest rates may reduce some consumers' purchasing power and desire or ability to spend, but those living on interest earnings will have increased earnings, hence may be more inclined to spend. The full effects on each part of the market will need to be considered. Rises in commodity prices may herald an increase in production costs and/or general inflation which will have a direct effect on a manufacturing business.

Secondly, a director must regularly get information on the key economic trends.

At this point many readers will be wondering just how they can find out what is going on in the economy and, even worse, how to interpret the information – but don't worry, help is at hand!

Industry magazines often report on the economic factors expected to influence the industry, so there is at least once source of help. Some companies employ their own economist; a one-page report to directors before meetings (or if this can't be done a brief presentation at the Board meeting) will help directors understand what is happening in the economy and how it might influence the company. An alternative or additional source is for the company's bankers to send each director a copy of the bank's own economists' view of the situation. This option is available to companies of all sizes, large or small, from a multinational trader to a local transport company; bankers are happy to provide this useful service free. These views will always be 'the shape of one man's opinion', but there is little practical alternative to getting an expert's view.

In a business sensitive to changes in foreign currency exchange rates, directors regularly received reports from a bank's economist. The views were generally in the right area. Incidentally, directors also received the views from an economist in another bank whose predictions always seemed to be wrong by about a year. It was a useful crosscheck!

Some professional associations and trade associations produce information on the economic factors influencing a particular industry. For some companies specific economic information may be essential. If a company's major raw material is copper, for example, the trend of prices is important. Companies with large borrowings or cash surpluses will pay attention to the forecast trend for interest rates. Banks or commodity dealers usually issue circulars that have a helpful discussion of the current and forecast market.

Directors are not expected to be economic experts, but do need to understand the trends which could affect the company, its results and strategy.

REPORTS ON THE COMPANY'S PERFORMANCE

KEY POINTS

This area is key to success. All Board reports on the company's actual performance must be:

◆ complete
◆ measured against targets
◆ circulated promptly.

Financial and operating performance reports

To be useful, the reports must show the full financial picture, which means including:

- profit and loss account
- balance sheet
- cash flow statement.

Each one should show actual figures compared with agreed targets and past performance.

These reports have the same name as the documents forming the company's Annual Accounts, but the regular reports to directors will not be in the summary format used in the Annual Accounts. A more detailed analysis of the figures is needed for items including all classifications of revenue and costs, detail for debtors current and overdue, asset purchases, etc. In addition operating information relating to the financial result is essential – for example:

- units produced
- units in stock
- units awaiting dispatch to customers
- units sold.

KEY POINT

Monetary figures come alive when they are related to what is actually happening in the business; financial figures alone will not give a complete picture.

The figures and statistics needed by directors vary business by business and the important or 'key' performance indicators need to be identified.

Key performance indicators for revenue can range over:

- revenue per available seat mile or available tonne kilometres (airline)
- sales per square metre (shop)
- revenue per machine hour (contract engineering)
- revenue per staff hour (consultancy)
- percentage of hotel rooms occupied (hotel).

Measures of costs might be:

- cost per staff member
- staff cost per square metre
- factory overhead per unit.

Balance sheet items also need to be measured, for example:

- debtors against sales – 'days of sales',
- inventories against production – 'days of production'.

There are many more. Each company and industry will have its own key performance indicators. It is important that the Board agree what performance indicators are essential for their company. The Company's chairman or chief executive officer can help a new director understand the significance of each ratio.

Small companies frequently do not pay sufficient attention to setting targets (budgets) and reporting actual results with the targets. The result of a recent survey in the UK, detailed on page 138, indicates a serious lack of information.

Financial key performance indicators are reviewed in more detail on page 112.

Forecasts

It is important to know what has happened in the company, but to make decisions just on past performance is like trying to drive a car by only looking in the rear view mirror. Directors need to have an intelligent assessment of what future results are likely to be; not just a mathematical projection, but a forecast based on an assessment of likely conditions. Included in the forecast must be not only the operating results (profit and loss account with operating data), but also balance sheets and cash flow statements. Too often managers feel that if a forecast shows profits, everything else will be all right, ignoring the need to fund new levels of inventories, repay debts, buy new machinery and/or recruit more staff. Directors need to ensure resources are available.

The results in the forecast should have the same key performance indicators as the historic figures. They are a very useful way to judge whether the company is moving forward.

How the forecast is made will depend on the industry. In some businesses future results can be estimated by monitoring work in progress or advanced bookings, in others each day is a new challenge for the salesforce! The more difficult it is to forecast, the more important it is to produce a forecast.

There is little point treating a forecast as certainty. It will be a guess, but it should be a well-informed guess. The effort involved in producing a forecast will be proportionate to its probable accuracy. Directors will have seen forecasts that are simply projections of current figures adding a percentage. Clearly no thought has gone into the figures beyond including a figure with a decimal to give the data an appearance of an accuracy which is just not there.

The period for the forecast will be driven by the nature of the business, but the minimum period should be for the following 12 months, and preferably beyond. A long-range view, minimum of five years, is particularly important for the management of funding – i.e. borrowings and solvency.

Whether the information in an Annual Account-type package will contain all the information directors need to monitor a company depends on the reporting standards of the company and the country. Additional schedules detailing operating information such as staff numbers, available hours and machine hours will probably be needed.

Financial exposure
Directors need to be aware of the financial exposures the company has, including:

- amount of debt and when it is due for repayment
- how much debt has a fixed interest rate
- how much debt has a variable interest rate
- amount and value of bonds and deposits.

If the medium-term forecast shows that scheduled loan repayments exceed cash resources in some years, directors need to be aware of the problem and ensure that it is being well handled.

Forecast foreign currency earnings and liabilities can also be important to some companies. It is too late to take protection after a foreign currency has devalued! When things go wrong in the area of financial exposures the results can be disastrous for the company. Surprisingly, some of the most spectacular losses arise in companies large and sophisticated enough to have the latest and best control systems.

> At a conference on the operations of Treasury Departments, the chairman of a well-respected company explained how their treasury team produced a summary of the company's net exposures at the end of each month, which was reviewed by the Board towards the end of the following month. A lot can happen in a month, not to say two. Up-to-date information is needed.

Customer surveys

Periodically the company will probably establish what its customers think of its products and level of service. This is frequently done through a survey of customers' views on price, product usefulness and reliability. In addition some indication will be gained by routinely reporting such items as the number of products returned and the amount spent for 'service under guarantee'.

The results of a customer survey become more useful if they contain comparisons of customers' reactions to competing products. In addition to surveying the company's customers, it is important to get the views of potential customers and those who prefer a competing product.

It is easy for a large company to commission a survey of consumers, but a smaller company may not have the resources. This does not mean that a small company can ignore its current and potential customers. There are ways for a small company to gauge reactions, e.g. telephoning regular customers, or for a month asking each customer to complete a simple form after each purchase.

The results of each customer survey should be reported to directors. There is not a usual or standard format for presenting this vital information. The results presented to the Board should include observations from the company's marketing department. Any business that does not stay in touch with its customers and understand what they think of the company, its products and services, is asking for trouble.

Staff surveys

Similarly, the attitude of staff to the company needs to be monitored. The goals and strategy of the company will be achieved through and by its staff. Staff must understand clearly what the company wants to achieve and what they need to do to meet the goals. Directors need to be confident that staff know and understand the company's objectives and are being given the training and facilities to achieve them.

In a small company the staff survey will probably consist of a summary of the reasons given by staff for leaving, with a summary of comments made by staff during their annual meeting with their manager. Yes, the process of communicating with staff is just as important in a small company as in a large one.

The staff turnover graph referred to on page 66 may show an early indication of a problem with staff morale. A significantly higher staff turnover rate than the industry's average can indicate that there is a problem.

Human resources is a difficult but important area. It is difficult because staff are people and people don't always say exactly what they mean and may comment in a way not fully understood by the listener. The results of a staff attitude survey will probably best be reported and interpreted to directors via the personnel manager or chief executive officer. Directors must see the results, but may need help to understand them fully.

One staff survey concluded that insufficient attention was paid to career development in the Finance Department, although there were detailed plans for individual staff identifying training needs and possible progression. After a lot of investigation it was established that the real problem was that some of the supervisors responsible for managing the staff were afraid of being frank with staff about the plans, in case there was a change and the staff were disappointed. Focused training for the managers overcame the problem.

How useful is the information?

The objective of all these reports is to give directors **information** which is **useful** and is **used** in running the business, not just lists of figures, however attractively presented.

In an operating company, estimated operating results were produced two days after the end of every week. A team of four staff produced the figures. All the managers found the report 'interesting', but admitted they did not actually use the figures when making decisions. The reports were discontinued.

The importance of measuring

It is a truism that 'what gets measured, gets managed'. Directors must know what has happened and what is likely to happen to the company's results and operating position, but there is still the question of whether this lines up with the company's longer term goals. 'This is where we are, that is where we are likely to be, *but is that where we want or need to be?'*.

The answer to this question will appear when comparing the key figures in performance reports with previously agreed long-range targets. This means having targets not just for the financial results and financial position, but the operating ratios, customer satisfaction, staff attitude and all key performance indicators.

Making a comparison with a company's own agreed targets is very important, but the process becomes even more useful if the report also includes comparisons with others in the same industry. It is often difficult to get comparative figures for competitors' performance against all measures, but a little information is better than none. The Annual Report of competitors may give some useful information, as may Chambers of Commerce. Too many business reports are inward looking, reporting only the company's own data. A business must be aware of how its competitors are performing.

How reports should be presented

Directors need to absorb and consider all of the information. They are responsible for the success of a company, the livelihood of its staff and to an extent, the success of its suppliers of goods and services.

There clearly is a danger of information overload. Similarly information may not be easy to understand.

There are many techniques for presenting information so it can be easily and quickly understood, such as:

◆ graphs (examples are shown on page 92)

◆ trend lines

◆ using bullet points for narrative.

Directors must be informed about the key parts of the business, but not every fine detail. It is not easy to produce a simple report for a complex business, but failure to do this will place a substantial burden on the directors, particularly the non-executive directors. The responsibility for producing concise reports rests with the company's management, but if the right information is not produced, the directors must make their demands clear and insist they are met.

A small business can experience the problem of not having the systems to produce sufficient information for directors to see what is going on. Fortunately systems are now available which will operate on a laptop computer and will, almost certainly, provide all the information directors need and in addition will present it in a

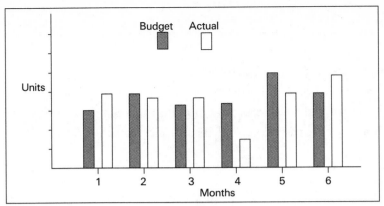

Graph

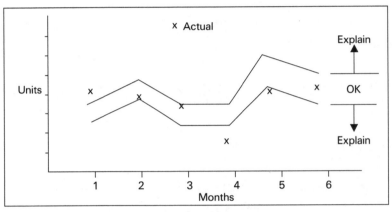

Control Chart

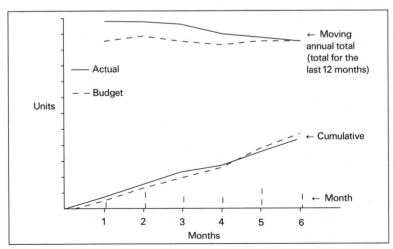

'Z' chart

variety of forms, e.g. 3D graphs.

If the managers do not themselves understand what the essentials of the business are, they are unlikely to be able to give focussed reports to their directors.

One useful guideline for the length of a report is that a director should be able to read and understand the complete report in two hours. This really defines the length of the report and sets quite a challenge to the producer.

Directors need to have the report in their hands with enough time to:

◆ read it
◆ raise queries and have them answered
◆ request that an item be added to the agenda for the next meeting, if necessary.

This means that reports need to be delivered to Board members at least one week before the Board meeting. The information a director should receive before a Board meeting is listed at the end of this chapter.

RESOLVING QUERIES BEFORE THE MEETING

It is very likely that while reviewing the information, a director will need to clarify some points. The easiest way to resolve these minor questions is for there to be a designated point of contact, a 'window' in the company responsible for answering questions from directors. This could be the chairman, but is more likely to be the chief executive officer, chief financial officer or company secretary. Not all companies like the 'one window' approach, in which case the Board will agree a list of directors (and senior managers) in the company who will answer directors' questions without going via the chairman.

If the answer clarifies the point the director will probably be satisfied, but it may be that the answer is not satisfactory or highlights an issue the director believes is important. In this case the director should discuss the matter with the chairman before the meeting to see whether it needs to be discussed by the full Board. It is the **type** of consideration that drives the timing for issuing reports to the Board.

Minor questions should be answered before the meeting. Few things are more irritating at a Board meeting than a director asking simple questions which could have been answered by a two-minute telephone call.

> **One director regularly held up discussion of the 'Results compared to Budget' while he added up the figures to make sure the totals were right. He did not last long on the Board, although I am sure he felt he was demonstrating to the rest of the Board a thorough approach!**

FREQUENCY OF BOARD MEETINGS

Many companies believe that a monthly Board meeting is essential and that it is a useful way to keep directors in the picture and build confidence between the executive and non-executive directors. In New Zealand the advice on best practice recommends '...meetings in each month of the year except January...'; Hong Kong a minimum of four each year. There is, however, a trend to less frequent meetings, perhaps three or four times a year, on the basis that this leaves the management free to get on with running the business and keeps directors focussed on important issues. There is no golden number of meetings; a Board must decide how often it needs to meet to do its job well. The number of meetings can change year by year if the company's needs change.

BOARD REPORTS

If the Board does not meet each month, Board reports should still be sent regularly (monthly) to all directors. Frequent distribution of information will help non-executive directors stay in touch with what is happening in the company.

Executive directors also need to see the total picture more frequently than at a quarterly Board meeting. Dealing every day with the operations of an area of a company does not leave much time to hear what is going on in other areas; monthly reports fill the gap.

MAJOR ISSUES ON THE AGENDA

In addition to regular reports on past performance, forecast performance and performance compared with strategic goals, directors need to receive early advice, before the Board meeting, of any major discussions or decisions that will be on the agenda for the meeting. 'Major' can cover any matter, e.g. a proposed management reorganisation, investment in new equipment, recommended changes to the remuneration structure for staff, buying another company – the list is almost endless.

The pre-meeting package sent to directors should include a briefing on these major issues detailing the thinking behind the proposal, its cost, desired outcome and possible alternatives. Directors should not be asked to make 'surprise' decisions either on major matters or simply to endorse management's recommendation.

> **One Board organised a special briefing meeting for directors when it was proposed to buy a major new range of operating equipment.**

KEY POINT

Directors should arrive at the Board meeting well briefed, with minor questions answered and a briefing on any major items on the agenda. Equally directors should allow themselves time to discuss the obvious!

> **A Board considering buying a new machine spent three quarters of an hour debating whether the purchase was worthwhile. This despite receiving a commitment from a major customer to buy a substantial part of the new machine's production as well as itself buying new machinery to integrate with the output of the new machine.**

'PRE-MEETING MEETING'

It is not unusual for all directors to meet informally before the formal Board meeting to talk over major issues. The objective of meeting is not to pre-empt the debate and discussion at the Board meeting, but to give directors a chance to seek clarifications, have technical terms explained and generally ensure that all aspects of an issue are fully understood. The issues in even a well written Board paper may not be fully understood by everybody. You may need further information before being able to evaluate a recommendation; it is sensible to know this and have the additional information available at the meeting when the decision is needed.

SUMMARY

◆ In a complex company, directors cannot get into detail.

◆ In a simpler company, directors must not get into detail.

◆ Approve concepts.

◆ Know the plans.

◆ The quality of information determines the Board's success.

◆ Avoid having too much information, stay with key information.

◆ Organise the presentation of information clearly.

◆ Do not look only at financial figures.

◆ Ask for the information needed to do the job.

INFORMATION DIRECTORS SHOULD RECEIVE REGULARLY.

◆ Background information on the industry and economy.
◆ Actual operating results compared to targets.
◆ Forecast operating results compared to long-term plans.
◆ Actual and forecast key performance indicators.
◆ Actual and forecast financial position.
◆ Actual and forecast financial exposure.
◆ Actual cashflow compared to forecast.
◆ Operating commentary from the chief executive officer and chief financial officer.
◆ Reports and recommendations from Board sub-committees.
◆ Detailed reports on any major items for discussion at the following meeting.

5

Getting to Grips with the Company's Finances

Shareholders have invested part of their wealth in the company;
employees invest their knowledge and part of their life. The
prosperity of suppliers depends to an extent on the company. Every
economy needs successful companies.

Directors need to understand how the company stands financially
and how it is financed. They have a particular duty to ensure that the
company is solvent. All decisions made by the Board eventually
have a financial effect on the company.

'BUT I'M NOT AN EXPERT IN FINANCE'

Directors are not expected to be expert in finance and accounting,
but must understand what has happened financially and what the
financial future may hold for the company.

Finance and accounting are described as 'the language of business'.
Any language must be learnt. All directors must have a working
knowledge of this important language; being expert in other
'languages', e.g. marketing, does not excuse any director from
speaking finance!

Getting help

There are people who will help a director understand a company's finances. The chief financial officer is there to help, as are the chairman and chief executive officer and the chairman of the company's Audit Committee. The company's auditors also stand ready to assist. Do not be shy about asking questions – a director has the right and duty to know what is going on.

ACCOUNTING POLICIES

Each year there are reports of 'creative accounting' – i.e. choosing accounting policies that produce the best result. The accounts are designed to reflect the truth. All directors, not just those on the Audit Committee, need to be convinced that each accounting policy truly reflects the way the business operates. The wrong accounting treatment will cause problems in all companies, small or large.

A large company has the resources to investigate, compare and evaluate various accounting treatments. A small company may feel it can do little and may not be able to afford to allocate funds to an investigation. There are a few options that are open:

- Discuss the problem with a trade association; they may have information on usual accounting practices in the industry.

- Each year ask the external auditor whether the accounting policies have been, and still are, appropriate.

- See what other companies in the same industry do.

It is possible to be active without spending a lot of money.

USES OF FINANCIAL DATA

'Money' figures are used in so many parts of a Board's operation. They are part of:

◆ setting strategic goals
◆ reviewing and agreeing budgets
◆ risk management
◆ monitoring operating performance
◆ reviewing progress towards long-term targets
◆ recommending dividends
◆ deciding whether a company is solvent

... the list goes on.

There are four types of Company financial statements:

◆ record of what has happened – **Statutory Accounts**
◆ statement of the current financial position – **Periodic Results**
◆ forecast of the financial position – **Monthly Results**
◆ analysis of financial exposures – **Position Report.**

DOUBLE ENTRY ACCOUNTING

The modern system of accounting is known as **double entry**. The advantages of the double entry approach are:

1. There is a complete record of each transaction.

2. The accounts contain full financial information, hence statements showing the achievements and the state of the company can be made.

3. The records cover all aspects of the business, making control easier and revealing trends.

4. There is a check on the arithmetic accuracy of the clerical process.

5. It is simple to understand.

The theory of double entry accounting is that a business transaction is a transfer of value between two people. This value may be in the form of money, goods or services. Usually goods or services will be exchanged for money. When the transaction takes place it is assumed that the values exchanged are equal, hence the exchange is balanced – thus the accounts recording the transaction also balance.

Underlying all accounting practices is the very basic idea of 'balance', which acknowledges that every transaction has at least two aspects and that the total of the value gained (an **asset**) is matched by a reduction in another asset and/or an increase in an amount owed (a **liability**).

Example 1

If a newly formed company issues shares for a total value of $1,000,000 the two entries will be:

- A 'plus', called a debit, to the 'bank' account of $1,000,000 for the amount received from shareholders because the amount in the company's bank account has increased.

- A 'minus' called a credit, to shareholders' funds of $1,000,000 because the shareholders are owed the amount they have paid to the company.

A **balance sheet**, i.e. a statement of the balance on all accounts, prepared after this one transaction, would show:

	$		$
Capital and Reserves	1,000,000	*Liquid Funds*	1,000,000
Total Liabilities	1,000,000	*Total Assets*	1,000,000

Applying the double entry approach ensures that the assets of the company equal its liabilities.

It should be remembered that the amount paid to the company by its shareholders and the profits not paid out to shareholders as dividends is treated as an amount owed to shareholders, hence a 'liability'.

Example 2

If the company then borrows $1,500,000 and uses $500,000 of its bank balance to buy a property for $2,000,000, there would be three bookkeeping entries, but the total of the pluses, 'debits', would still equal the total of the minuses, 'credits'.

A balance sheet produced at this stage would show:

	$		$
Capital and Reserves	1,000,000	*Fixed Assets*	2,000,000
Bank Loan	1,500,000	*Liquid Funds*	500,000
Total Liabilities	2,500,000	*Total Assets*	2,500,000

The transactions and the accounts are still 'in balance'.

The examples above show the principle and deals with financing assets. The principle is the same for operations, when the results are shown in the profit and loss account.

Example 3

If the company takes goods, which cost $150,000, from stock, employs a contractor to customise them at a cost of $40,000 and sells them for $220,000, the entries are:

Increase, Liquid Funds by	$220,000	} (sale)
Increase, Profit and Loss by	$220,000	
Reduce, Stocks by	$150,000	}(cost of sale)
Reduce, Profit and Loss by	$150,000	
Reduce, Liquid Funds by	$40,000	}(contractor)
Reduce, Profit and Loss by	$40,000	

The balance in the Profit and Loss account will be a profit of $30,000 ($220,000 − ($150,000 + $40,000)).

A balance sheet produced at this stage would show:

	$		$
Capital	1,000,000	Fixed Assets	2,000,000
Reserves			
Profit and Loss	30,000	Repaid Funds	530,000
Bank loan	1,500,000		
Total Liabilities	2,530,000	Total Assets	2,530,000

Accounting really does not need to become much more complicated than this.

The position becomes clearer when looked at through the financial statements a director will read regularly.

STATUTORY ACCOUNTS

These are the reports the law requires a company to produce. These comprise as a minimum:

- **balance sheet** – the company's financial position on a date
- **profit and loss account** – the financial result achieved in the period
- **cash flow statement** – summary of cash received and paid in the period.

A company may produce Statutory Accounts once each year for the year, each six months for the half year or each quarter. In all circumstances a set of Statutory Accounts must be produced for each full year.

The actual format of the Statutory Accounts varies substantially from country to country depending on legal requirements and best practice. All companies in a country will use the same basic formats; some producing just the minimum, others including additional information.

Balance sheet

This portrays the Company's financial position as at a certain date; a snapshot.

The statement will show:

- how much the company owes and is owed
- value of assets owned
- whether the company is solvent, i.e. can pay its debts as they become due
- value of the shareholders' investment in the company.

For an example of a simple balance sheet see opposite.

	Year 2	Year 1
	$	$
NON CURRENT ASSETS		
Fixed Assets	186,870	183,400
Intangible Assets	37,100	43,750
Investments	70,000	70,000
TOTAL	293,970	297,150
CURRENT ASSETS		
Stock	32,904	32,070
Debtors	26,806	25,874
Bank	9,731	7,786
TOTAL	69,441	65,730
TOTAL ASSETS	363,411	362,880
CURRENT LIABILITIES		
Current portion of Bank Loan	6,000	6,000
Creditors	28,841	29,430
Taxes	5,390	5,500
Proposed dividend	2,640	2,450
TOTAL	42,871	43,380
NON CURRENT LIABILITIES		
Bank Loan	87,500	89,000
TOTAL LIABILITIES	130,371	132,380
CAPITAL & RESERVES		
Share Capital	100,000	100,000
Reserves	133,040	130,500
TOTAL SHAREHOLDERS' FUNDS	233,040	230,500

Example of a balance sheet

Note:	Total Assets	363,411	362,880
	less Total Liabilities	130,371	132,380
	Shareholders Funds	233,040	230,500

What the headings mean:

Assets	What the company owns
Bank	Money the bank owes to the company
Bank Loan	Amount owed to banks repayable after 12 months excluding the current portion
Creditors	Amount owed to suppliers
Current portion of Bank Loan	Amount of bank loans due to be repaid in the next 12 months
Debtors	Money owed to the company
Fixed Assets	Physical assets – you can see them
Intangible Assets	Rights owned – you can't see them
Investment	Money invested in another company
Liabilities	Amounts owed to others
Non Current Assets	Assets the company plans to own for many years
Proposed Dividend	Share of the profits the directors recommend paying to shareholders
Reserves	The balance of profits not paid to share holders
Share Capital	Amount shareholders have invested in the company
Stocks (Inventory)	Goods for sale
Taxes	Amount owed to the government

KEY POINT

The balance sheet shows directors the current financial position of the company, permits measurement of financial management and will help to show whether the company is solvent.

Profit and loss account or income statement

This shows the result of a period's operations.

Example of a simple profit and loss account

	Year 2	Year 1
	$	$
REVENUE	105,158	100,380
− OPERATING EXPENSES	94,362	88,528
OPERATING PROFIT	10,796	11,852
− FINANCE COSTS	3,780	4,227
+ INCOME FROM INVESTMENTS	2,974	2,105
PROFIT BEFORE TAX	9,990	9,730
− TAX	4,810	4,780
PROFIT AFTER TAX	5,180	4,950
− DIVIDENDS	2,640	2,450
RETAINED PROFIT FOR THE YEAR	2,540	2,500

The figures are produced on the basis of 'accruals' – that is, each transaction is recorded when it happens, not when the money moves. For example, revenue is the amount invoiced to customers whether or not the cash has been received.

What the headings mean:

Dividends Share of profits the directors recommend paying to shareholders

Finance Costs Cost of money borrowed, reduced by any interest earned

	Year 2 $	Year 1 $
NET OPERATING CASH FLOW	15,525	23,213
INVESTMENT INCOME	2,980	2,008
LOAN INTEREST	3,820	4,155
TAX	4,920	4,280
INVESTING ACTIVITIES		
Assets Sold	7,000	8,000
Assets Bought	10,870	20,600
NET CASH FLOW BEFORE FINANCE		
FINANCING		
Loan Repayments	6,500	6,000
New Finance	5,000	10,000
DIVIDENDS PAID	2,450	2,400
CHANGES IN CASH (Increase)	1,945	5,786
CASH AT THE PERIOD END	9,731	7,786

Example of a cashflow statement

Income from Investments	Earnings from an investment in other companies
Operating Expenses	Costs incurred to make the products sold
Operating Profit	Surplus from selling the products
Retained Earnings	Balance of profits kept in the business
Revenue	Total amount invoiced for sales, sometimes called 'turnover'
Tax	Amount due to the government on the period's results.

Cash flow statement

This is a summary of the cash movements during the period. Over the long term 'profits' will equal 'cash', but in the short term this is not always so.

> **'Understand the cash. Accounting entries can be manipulated; cash cannot.'**

What the headings mean:

Assets Bought	Cost of assets bought
Assets Sold	Sale proceeds of assets sold
Cash at the Period End	A statement of the actual amounts at the end of the period; this is the result of adjusting the balance at the beginning of the period by the 'Changes in Cash'
Changes in Cash	The net effect of all cash transactions

Financing	Transactions relating to the financing of the business
Investing activities	Dealings in assets
Investment income	Dividends received from investments
Loan interest	Interest paid and received
Loan repayments	Amount of loans repaid
Net operating cash flow	Cash received from the company's operations
New finance	Amount of new loans received
Tax	Taxes paid.

KEY POINT

Attached to all three statements will be schedules with **Notes to the Accounts** explaining the figures in more detail.

The reported Operating Profit is a significantly different figure to the Net Operating Cash Flow, i.e. the cash inflow from operating activities. To help the reader understand the differences it is usual to include in the accounts a '**Reconciliation of Operating Profit to Net Cash Inflow from Operating Activities**'. The statement tracks and details the difference between the Operating Profit and the Net Operating Cash Flow. Essentially the difference between the two figures are the non-cash charges, e.g. depreciation. It also eliminates calculated figures, e.g. profit on disposal of an associated company. The cash inflow from the sale is in the cash flow statement. The profit is the difference between the value of the associated company in the accounts and the sale price achieved.

One of the problems with understanding Statutory Accounts (and hence the monthly results) is that some of the bases used to prepare them do not always seem to be logical. Many accountants would agree! These bases are called **Accounting Standards**. They are like the rules of grammar in a language and are usually set by a national professional organisation. National Accounting Standards only cover major accounting transactions. In addition a company will have its own accounting policies that describe how all transactions are recorded. The most common standards and policies are:

♦ **Going Concern**. The assumption that the company will continue to operate for at least one more year and has the ability to meet all its obligations as they become due. This means that the value of assets, e.g. buildings, are recorded at their original cost. If the company is not expected to last another year the basis will change to 'Liquidation' and expected sale values will be used.

♦ **Consistently Applied Accounting Principles**. The company's accounting policies this year are unchanged from those of last year. If there is a change, the financial effect will be calculated and included as a Note to the Accounts.

♦ **Materiality**. All material items have been included, i.e. some non-material amounts or adjustments may not be included. There is nothing sinister in this. It may be that the company has a dispute with a supplier and is not able to assess accurately what the outcome will be. Materiality will generally be judged as any amount less than 5% of Profit or less than 10% of Total Assets.

♦ **Anticipate Losses not Profits**. Not often stated as a policy, but nevertheless applied in most cases. A conservative approach where potential losses are recorded immediately, e.g. making an allowance for debtors who will never pay, for whatever reason; but any potential profits are not recorded until they are certain, e.g. from the forward sale of foreign currencies.

In addition to understanding these conventions, directors must get to grips with the company's accounting policies. These explain how the company records major transactions, e.g. how the depreciation charge is calculated. This is a wide area and a new director should discuss accounting policies with the chief financial officer and the chairman of the Audit Committee. If the policies are complex or difficult, the Company's auditors should be included in the discussion.

> **'Big profits you don't understand are more dangerous than large losses you do.'**

REPORT FORMATS

The primary objectives of a report are to:

- communicate information clearly
- highlight important information
- put information into a context.

The user should decide the content and format of a report. This principal applies equally to shareholders as to company managers. The minimum content of the Statutory Accounts will be detailed in company law, but this is a minimum and other information should be added to help the reader.

There is more flexibility in the design of company management reports.

In all cases charts and graphs can help the reader understand the information. Comparisons with the industry, other companies and targets also help.

The content and format of reports should be reviewed regularly, at least once each year. There are many useful techniques that will help improve the value of a report.

RATIOS

The total monetary figures included in the Statutory Accounts permit the reader to make some assessment of management's efficiency in running the business. There are a series of standard ratios that can be used for this purpose. These calculations use the figures in the previous accounts.

		Year 2	Year 1
Return on Equity	Profit after Tax	2.22%	2.15%
	Total Shareholders' Funds		
Return on Assets	Profit after Tax	1.43%	1.36%
	Total Assets		
Sales Margin	Operating profit	10.27%	11.81%
	Revenue		
Quick Ratio	Current Assets less Stocks	0.85	0.78
	Current Liabilities		
Cash Flow	Net Operating Cash Flow	11.91%	17.54%
	Total Liabilities		
Gearing Ratio	Total Loans	1:0.40	1:0.41
	Total Shareholders' Funds		
Interest Cover	Profit before Interest and Tax	3.64	3.30

	Finance Cost		
Asset Turnover	Revenue	0.289	0.277
	Total Assets		
Growth	This Year's Revenue	4.76%	
	Last Year's Revenue		

These results are an illustration only; they are not for a real company. If they were actual results, the directors would be concerned at the low rate of return on equity (shareholders' funds) and total assets. The return is less than the cost of borrowing, so the banks are getting a better return than the shareholders. Assets 'turn over' once in three years; it is likely that the company has too much money invested in assets and in assets that are not producing a return higher than the cost of borrowing.

The company's investments produced a return of a little more than 3% in Year 1 (2105/70000) and about 4.25% in Year 2 (2974/70000). These ratios are good indicators of where directors should start to look for ways to improve the performance of the Company.

The **financial ratios** and **financial key performance indicators** can be very helpful to directors:

◆ enabling comparisons to be made with other companies and other industries

◆ highlighting the trend of important figures over years

◆ eliminating or mitigating the effects of monetary inflation

◆ establishing a relationship between figures, e.g. revenue and finance costs

◆ judging whether business plans and budgets include an improvement in the management of the company's finances.

There are many more financial ratios and measures that can be used. Care is always needed when trying to use ratios, and financial ratios are no exception. You need to be clear of the differences between the terms that can be used – e.g. 'Net Profit Attributable to Shareholders', 'Profit Before Tax', 'Profit Before Tax And Exceptional Items', 'Earnings Before Interest, Tax and Amortisations (EBITA)' – and the many others which are used regularly and the new ones that are introduced periodically. Not all are appropriate to every company or every industry; e.g. the 'Quick Ratio' is not always helpful where a company such as an airline has substantial bank loans secured against assets. The 'Gearing Ratio' is not helpful to a cargo sales agent that does not borrow. It is impossible to give universal rules and guidance. The Board under the guidance of the chairman should discuss and decide which are the useful ratios. Ratios make financial figures more 'real' and understandable. Measurement is an aid to management, not a substitute.

Financial ratios are not the only measures directors need to see (see page 83).

The company's chief financial officer and the chairman of the Audit Committee are the best people to explain how the accounting policies and accounting standards are applied in the company's accounts and their effect. Directors must understand the figures and what they mean. There is no excuse for not doing so; it is not difficult, even accountants can do it!

Often the wording and layout of financial statements does not encourage people to read them, but at the end of the day success or failure will be judged on the 'numbers', so you need to have a working knowledge of them. If the financial statements are difficult to understand, perhaps a new director can help by suggesting ways to make them more intelligible to the Board as well as to the person on the street.

Boards frequently have an Audit Committee made up of non-executive directors with the job of monitoring the Statutory Accounts and discussing them with the company's auditors. Having this committee does not relieve the other directors from the responsibility of understanding the figures and their implications.

Most sets of Statutory Accounts include a Chairman's Statement in which the chairman reviews the happenings, good and bad, of the past year and discusses the result. The review should also assess the current trading situation and look forward to the likely result for the coming year. This is an important communication statement. Surveys have concluded that the Chairman's Statement is the only part of the Statutory Accounts everyone reads! All directors should contribute to agreeing the contents of the statement; it is not sufficient to leave the contents solely to the chairman, chief executive officer or chief financial officer. Don't be frightened to mention problems or failures as well as successes.

PERIODIC PERFORMANCE REPORTS

Regularly, usually monthly, directors will receive a report of the company's results. The format will be similar to the Statutory Accounts, but supported by more detail and including operating figures and comparisons with the agreed budget (business plan). Although the formats vary greatly by company and industry, the basics needed are constant.

Example of a periodic performance report

SALES – JANUARY

Product	Actual		Budget		Analysis of difference in value, due to:				
	Units	Value	Units	Value	Units		Price		Total
	$	$	$	$	$	$	$	$	$
					Bad	Good	Bad	Good	
A	132	660	125	750		42	132		−90
B	57	3,534	60	3,780	189		57		−246
C	3,764	22,584	3,500	21,000		1,584			+1,584
Total		26,778		25,530					+1,248

The basis for calculating the 'difference in value' is:

Units – (Budgeted units – Actual units) × budgeted selling price
Price – (Budgeted price – Actual price) × actual units

This presentation prompts some questions directors may want to ask:

- Products A and B failed to achieve the required price level. Why?
- Sales of Product A were more than was planned but at a lower price. Has the market changed?
- Sales of Product C were substantially more than planned and were at budgeted prices. Is this due to a change in customers' buying habits ?

Some companies only produce a profit and loss account with

operating information to directors. This is not sufficient information; at the least a balance sheet and a cash flow statement are needed to complete the picture.

A recent article in the magazine *Financial Management* commented that small companies generally do not budget or report regularly using all three financial statements. Fewer than 40% regularly report the actual figures for the balance sheet and cash flow, although a greater number budget them. This is a serious omission. Most small companies budget their bank balance, but not all compare the actual position with the budget. Small companies need to have a firm grip on their overall financial position. In some ways it is easier for larger companies to achieve the right level of monitoring, but modern accounting systems are available and affordable for any size of company.

EFFICIENCY MEASURES

In addition to money and operating figures, reports should include ratios measuring efficiency compared to budget. There are three basic types of efficiency measures:

- **high level**, attempting to measure overall performance, e.g. number of customers served, average amount spent by each customer

- **operating efficiency**, highlighting how well the unit is operating, e.g. customers served each staff hour, average time a customer was waiting to be served

- **areas of concern**, focussing on parts of the operation that have problems, e.g. comparing efficiency ratios between locations.

Care is needed when selecting measures – use the wrong ones and the company will get a misleading answer.

In the late 1950s, when the USSR was a centrally planned economy, there was a report of the result of using the wrong efficiency measures. To improve efficiency in shoe production, factories' targets were set only in units. Factories met these targets by producing only either left or right shoes. Sadly 75% of factories opted to produce left-footed shoes. Hardly the desired or comfortable outcome.

There is sometimes a distinction made between financial and non-financial measures or key performance indicators. They are equally important: money is one side of the coin, efficiency the other. Non-financial key performance indicators help people understand the money, but are not a substitute for financial measures.

Total money figures are important, but they come to life when they are measured against operating information, e.g. sales per square metre, cost per operating hour. In general there need be no more than a total of ten or twelve high level and operating measures. These efficiency measures should be compared regularly with others in the same industry and in similar industries. Performance reports should not only look inward at the company's own result.

FORECASTS

The monthly results should also include a forecast for the remainder of the year and beyond. In addition to reviewing what has happened, directors must look ahead. Realistic forecasts allow directors to have some forewarning of problems. Almost every change, whether good or bad, produces a problem:

slow down in sales (bad) = problems with cash control and profitability.

rapid growth in sales (good) = problems with finding resources, e.g. cash, people.

Directors should be alert to the assumptions used in forecasts and the way they are presented.

> A company had a 'cost overrun system' where actual costs more than 10% over budget were reported to the Board. What the Board did not realise was that once the overspend had been reported it was incorporated into the budget and did not appear on subsequent reports. The company had cost overruns in excess of $1 million, a substantial amount for the company.

Directors must interpret the figures and ratios and judge the efficiency of the operations. The figures and ratios may show worrying trends, e.g. increases in the value of Stocks and Debtors while sales decrease.

SOLVENCY

This is an important area for directors to monitor. Indications of a problem looming will come from the financial figures, the financial ratios and long-term cash flow forecast. Poor financial performance always produces problems.

In addition there are non-financial warning signs. Many business books give lists of what to watch for. These can be very helpful to a director. For example, look out for:

- suppliers frequently chasing overdue payments
- increasing credit period taken from suppliers
- treasury staff becoming too busy to produce cash forecasts
- assets appearing in the balance sheet which should be written off
- changes to accounting policies that change losses into profits, e.g. capitalising operating costs
- financial information that is not up to date.

This information may not jump immediately out of any particular report. The simple way to get it is to ask questions at the Board meeting.

FINANCIAL POSITION REPORT

Some directors believe that their responsibility stops with understanding the company's financial and performance reports. This is not true. Directors need to understand the company's full financial position and what 'exposures' there are.

KEY POINT
Exposure = Risk = 'Any circumstance that will adversely affect the company and its results'.

Changes in financial markets affect all organisations. Often there are good and bad aspects to the same change, e. g. a rise in interest rates will increase the cost to borrowers, but increase the income of those with money on deposit, hence their ability to spend. Changes in foreign exchange rates can directly affect costs or income. Directors must also consider whether the change will make a competitor's product more or less price attractive. It could be that changes in commodity prices should also be monitored.

Directors need to understand how financial exposures are managed and need to be comfortable with the approach taken. There is not an ideal or right way to manage exposures – e.g. borrowing at a fixed interest rate in order to know the intersest cost means that a company cannot benefit from a fall in rates. The board needs to endorse the strategy for managing financial risks. A simple report sent to directors regularly will help.

Example of a financial exposures report

FINANCIAL EXPOSURES – JANUARY
INTEREST RATE RISK

Amount by Bank	Currency			Interest	Type Millions		Total
	£GBP	$USD	€euro	Rate	Fixed	Variable	Owed
ABC	100			4.1%	100		100
DEF			70	3.7%		70 ⎫	120
DEF		50		4.5%	50	⎬	
GHI		100		4.9%		100 ⎭	100
TOTAL	100	150	70		150	170	320

This statement will give the totals due in different currencies (foreign exchange rate risk), amounts due to different banks (establishment risk) and amount borrowed with fixed and variable interest rates (interest rate risk). Similar figures should be produced for funds invested.

Where a company has a significant exposure to foreign currencies, a cash forecast in each of the major foreign currencies will help directors understand how much is at risk. A routine report might include:

FOREIGN EXCHANGE RATE RISK – JANUARY

Currency   (our currency)

	Month Due	1	2	3	Etc. >
£GBP	Receivable	10,000	11,000	9,500	
	Payable	7,450	7,000	6,900	
	Net	2,550	4,000	2,600	
$USD	Receivable	13,250	10,000	11,000	
	Payable	10,050	510	7,650	
	Net	3,200	9,490	3,350	

This report shows when foreign currency surpluses are forecast to arise. A separate report will list an action taken to manage the risk.

Risk management

Financial risks are one set of the risks facing a company – there are others. The responsibility for all risk management stays with the Board of Directors. The Board may ask a committee or an individual director to look at the issues in detail, but the Board as a whole is responsible for ensuring that the process is sound.

Directors are not expected to be omnipotent, but are required to act in the same way as a prudent person and treat the company's financial affairs with as much care as their own!

IN CONCLUSION

Finance is part of each director's responsibility. The figures give a useful insight into the workings of the company. It can appear to be an intimidating subject, but with perseverance directors can become comfortable with it. Finance and accounting is the language of business, and directors need to speak it well!

A little learning is a dangerous thing. The information provided here will not make a director a financial expert; it just gives the basics. The next step is further reading and a talk with the company's chief financial officer.

SUMMARY

It is essential that directors invest the time to understand an organisation's financial system, reports and exposures and also how the financial results relate to the operation of the business via key performance indicators.

◆ Financial reports are an essential way of showing the result of operations and the financial health of an operation.

◆ All directors must understand how the figures are prepared and what they mean.

◆ Ratios and measurers make the total money figures come to life.

◆ Comparisons need to be made to past performance, the last forecast, others in the industry and competitors.

◆ Reports on current operations and forecast future results are needed regularly.

◆ Directors need regularly to see the detail of a company's financial exposures.

◆ Be clear about the company's current and future solvency position.

6

How a Board Meeting Works

Why do the directors meet regularly? Why come together as a committee or 'Board'? Why get together at all?

Whether 'more is better' is an interesting debate. A survey of companies in Hong Kong's Hang Seng Index – Hong Kong's biggest public companies – made by the Hong Kong Institute of Directors in November 1998 noted a wide range in the size of boards. The smallest Board had seven directors and the largest 23 directors plus three advisors. The approximate spread was:

25% 10 directors or less
50% 11 to 16 directors
25% 16 or more directors

Compare this with the averages in the Higgs report (page 130). The overall average for UK listed companies is 6.7 directors.

The Board exists to achieve an objective: the success of the business. The size needs to be appropriate to the needs of the business and the size of the task – not very precise advice, but about all that can sensibly be said. General management advice and common sense suggests that a workable size for any committee is six to eight people and this logic applies to a Board as well.

ALLOCATION OF RESPONSIBILITIES

KEY POINT

The purpose of the Board of Directors is to ensure the company's prosperity by collectively directing its affairs.

To achieve this directors must be clear what responsibilities remain with the Board of Directors and what duties have been delegated to operating management. It is preferable that this separation is in writing. The Statement of Board Reserved Powers (see page 57) lists the responsibilities a Board keeps for itself.

Operating management

The duties of the operating management (including the executive directors) should be formally delegated to the chief executive officer (or whatever other title the chief executive has). These might include:

- Implement all plans, policies and strategies approved by the Board within the timetable agreed.

- Submit regular progress reports to the Board on the implementation of approved plans, policies and strategies.

- Effectively run the daily operations of the company.

- Submit regular reports to the Board on the actual operations of the company compared to targets agreed by the Board.

- Be responsible for the daily financial management of the company.

For some items it is sensible for the Board to set limits on the authority of the chief executive officer, e.g. '...and may not commit the company to capital expenditure of more than $xxxx on any one project or $yyyy in any one financial year, without the prior approval of the Board'.

The list will also include items for staff management as well as compliance with legal requirements. It will be as long and detailed as the Board decides.

The Board's responsibilities

The Board is responsible for monitoring the company's day-to-day operations, but must resist the temptation of trying to resolve current problems. Stated in the simplest terms, the function of the Board is to look towards tomorrow, defining what 'success' will mean for the company and deciding what the company must do to be successful. To help achieve this the Board needs to know what is going on today, but their focus is the company's tomorrow.

The Board is responsible for monitoring progress towards strategic objectives, the implementation of its policies and adherence to business plans. Business plans are the detailed tactics which, if successful, will result in the company achieving its long-term goals.

In addition the Board has to monitor whether the organisation is complying with its legal and fiduciary (trustee or stewardship) obligations.

When information needs to be released to a stock exchange or to shareholders, directors must have enough time to understand and consider the wording of the report. Reviewing a complex announcement or report at the Board meeting can be extremely difficult and needs to be well organised. Directors will recall that for public companies, Stock Exchange Listing Rules specify what information needs to be released. If the matter is complex, directors will need to consider carefully the final wording of circulars to be issued by the Board.

> A public company wanted to complete a deal very quickly. The Stock Exchange required that a circular explaining the deal be sent to all shareholders. To save time directors were asked to approve a draft circular, which had several significant blanks with the explanation that, 'the lawyers will fill in the blanks, this is the way it's always done'. I am pleased to say that the directors declined to agree the wording until all details were final and included. The deal was completed on schedule.

All directors are responsible for taking a long-term view for the company, solving tomorrow's problems without becoming bogged down in today's issues. Clear allocation of responsibilities between the Board and management is important.

THE DAY TO DAY

Unfortunately directors are (or at least tend to be) human! There is a strong tendency and temptation for directors to chase and focus on the exciting, rather than the boring. The next deal is always more interesting than the problems of implementing the last. A strong chairman is needed to control any tendency to be drawn into the immediate, rather than the strategic, issues.

There is a frequent debate about the pros and cons of the two ways to organise company direction. The options are; unitary (one Board) and the bicameral (two Boards, one executive and one supervisory). I worked most of my life with unitary Boards. Through recent involvement with the bicameral approach, I now see the significant advantages of the bicameral approach:

- clear definition of the responsibilities between the two Boards
- formal reporting by the Executive Board to the Supervisory Board
- the Supervisory Board's need to review and approve the actions of the Executive Board.

These requirements are not formalities, but good 'checks and balances' and they do tend to keep the Supervisory Board away from routine issues.

BALANCE ON THE BOARD

The Board will thrive by having a mixture of skills and experience drawn from different and relevant backgrounds. A majority of directors with the same specialist knowledge, such as marketing, would be overkill, let alone several accountants or lawyers. There are books on ways to achieve 'balance' on the Board.

A balance of executive directors, non-executive directors and independent non-executive directors is important. A Board is a group of individual human beings; hence each works in a different way. It is not sensible to try to generalise. However, too many executive directors on a Board can produce a narrow operating focus. It is sometimes difficult for an executive director to think objectively about their own performance and the performance of their fellow executive directors.

> **It has been commented, 'One of the problems of a Board dominated by executive directors is that they are marking their own examination paper.'**

The Higgs Report mentioned the average composition of the Boards of listed companies in the UK.

	Chairman	Directors		
		Executive	Non-Executive	Total
FTSE 100	1.0	4.5	6.0	11.5
FTSE 250	1.0	4.0	4.0	9.0
Other listed	1.0	2.8	2.3	6.1
Grand Total	1.0	3.0	2.7	6.7

A large company may have some flexibility with the number and cost of directors, but it can be a difficult problem for a smaller company. Directors of a small company earn their fees and contribute as much as directors of larger companies, but the cost of each additional director can increase costs significantly. A Board of two or three directors can work perfectly well in a small company, but at least one should be non-executive.

There is also the need to balance experience gained through years in general business and an industry with an understanding of the potential of the latest ideas and thinking. The Hong Kong Institute of Directors 1998 survey summarised information on the length of service of directors, for those companies that report the information. The survey showed the length of time the longest-serving director had been on the Board:

91% of companies	at least one director, 11 years or more
55% of companies	at least one director, 20 years or more
21% of companies	at least one director, 30 years or more

The characterisations frequently attributed to executive directors and non-executive directors can be misleading. Theory says that executive directors possess the detailed knowledge of the industry and company and this narrow focus is balanced by the less detailed but wider experience of non-executive directors. There are many real-life circumstances where a non-executive director, who is perhaps a practising professional and has been on the Board for many years, knows more about the industry than a newly appointed executive director.

An article in the UK's *Evening Standard* discussing Boards in the USA and UK commented '...more non-executive directors, as in the American model, does not automatically mean better governance...The norm in America is for the Chief Executive and the Finance Director to be the only Executive Directors, with the remainder of places taken by Non-Executive outsiders. British executives with experience of the US system say it makes it even harder for Non-Executives to form an independent judgement because everything they are told is filtered through the Chief Executive. The weakness of governance in this country (UK) is the peculiar British desire to excessive politeness.'

The Board should not be misled by titles and formulae. It is axiomatic that the chairman and the Board ensure the Board has all the attributes, skills and experience it needs, and uses them all to the fullest. The effective operation and composition of Boards must be regularly reviewed (see pages 139 and 175) to ensure they meet the needs of the company.

The management team of executive directors is likely to be a more closely-knit unit than the non-executive members of the Board. The non-executive directors (only) may wish to meet informally before the Board meeting to discuss the Board's performance and any matters that concern them. Other Boards meet informally after the Board meeting. The format is not important; building a team is (see also 'pre-meeting meeting' on page 96).

It is helpful for all Board members to have the chance to meet informally to discuss matters of general interest, if only to help build all the individuals on the Board into one team. A Board will fail to meet its objectives if communication amongst directors is not clear, frank and open. A divided Board will not be able to develop and explain the company's strategy and the problems needing resolution.

> Sun Tsu wrote 'He whose ranks are united in purpose will be victorious.'

BOARD WORK PLAN

Before deciding the agenda for an individual meeting, the Board should have agreed a work plan for a full 12 months and keep it rolling into the year ahead. A list of the items in an annual plan is on page 134. Some items will appear for each meeting e.g.: Review forecast financial position, others at an appropriate time during the year, e.g.:

January	Review company strategy
	Review budgeting process
April	Compare financial and operating performance with competitors
July	Consider customer satisfaction survey
	Review staff satisfaction survey
October	Review board performance.

The plan should list the date, time and location of each Board meeting and the items scheduled to be discussed. This practice means that the agenda for the next meeting will be the items on the Board's agreed work plan, adjusted for any new matters needing attention.

The workload of the Board will vary meeting by meeting and with the time of the year, to meet the need of the company. The chairman, working with the chief executive and the company secretary, usually finalises the agenda for a Board meeting.

Not all Board meetings will deal with matters of high drama and strategy. The chairman, together with the Board, need to plan their work so that discussions and decisions are spread through the year and arise at the 'right' time.

When preparing the next 12 months' work plan the chairman and all directors should try to equalise the amount of work required to be completed at each meeting. However, this is the ideal and it is unlikely in practice that an even workload will be achieved. Directors have to be prepared to work longer at certain times of the year. The chairman is responsible for ensuring that adequate time is allocated for discussion of all the items on the agenda. If it is likely that a meeting will exceed the usual time, the directors should, if possible, be warned in advance. It is important that each agenda is discussed fully, not that the meeting is finished within a certain time. The needs of the business are the over-riding consideration.

Regular items on the Board's annual plan of work will be:

◆ Approve annual budget or profit plan.

◆ Review and approve Interim and Annual Accounts and Share-holders Report.

◆ Decide on interim dividends and recommend a final dividend for the year.

◆ Review the policies for marketing, customer relations, product development, personnel, finance, investor relations, social responsibility, health and safety.

◆ Review customer satisfaction surveys.

◆ Examine the survey of staff morale and satisfaction.

◆ Review reports and recommendations from the Board's committees.

◆ Review the company's current and forecast operating and financial performance.

◆ Review financial and operating risk exposures.

◆ Examine actual performance against goals.

- Approve communication with stakeholders, particularly share-holders, staff and bankers and ensure that strategy and the results achieved are communicated to them.

- Approve senior management remuneration.

The Board's work plan should include time to review past decisions. Decisions are made to achieve a purpose – the Board must establish whether the objective has been secured; it must monitor its own performance. Making a decision, announcing it and allocating resources does not mean that the decision will be fully carried out or will achieve the desired purpose.

> The Board agreed a manager's solution to a problem and allocated funds to implement it. A review a year later revealed that the manager had used the funds in another way in an attempt to achieve the same result. The problem had not been solved. The manager left the company.

The Board should be involved in the distribution of any share of the profits to staff including executive directors. There is a strong relationship between cash or share bonuses that are related to recent profit performance and the success of a company. This is a key motivational issue.

Board work plans in smaller companies

Some of these may seem to be just 'big company' matters – a small company may not need a series of Board sub-committees, but the functions of the committees still need to be handled in other ways (see page 28). Small companies do need a policy on customer relations and

and feedback from their customers on product service and reliability, even if it is only from a simple form given to each customer.

Minor changes may be needed to the plan for a smaller company that does not issue Interim Accounts or pay interim dividends. It may be that the shareholders are all directors, hence there is not a need to communicate agreed strategy, but there is still the need to communicate with other staff, etc.

CIRCULATING INFORMATION

The agenda, once agreed, should be circulated to all directors before the Board meeting and accompanied by:

- reports on finance and operations
- forecast results, both financial and operating
- papers from executive directors and other senior management on the major points.

Directors should be able to study major proposals before they meet as a Board. Not all reports will be ready when the agenda is sent to directors – those missing can be sent later, but the company should establish a discipline that all information for the meeting will be in directors' hands by a specific time before the meeting. The general practice is to set a time limit of between two and seven days; as a working director I prefer to have everything seven days before the meeting.

REVIEWING MINUTES

An early item on each Board agenda will be to review and approve the minutes of the last meeting. This is the last opportunity a director has to agree, or correct, what has been written for the company's permanent records. This is important as minutes can sometimes, almost miraculously, mention issues that not everybody believes were discussed, agreements that were not reached (although some directors think they were) and comments that a director only intended to make.

It is a good practice for the draft minutes to be approved by the chairman and circulated to all directors the day following the Board meeting. Challenges to the content of the minutes should be made before the meeting, through the chairman, not during the meeting.

THE ANNUAL BUDGET

Often the most difficult and time consuming areas for the Board are reviewing and agreeing the annual budget or plan and agreeing the Annual Report to Shareholders.

KEY POINT

The annual budget is a vital part of the process of achieving long-term goals.

The difference between what can be achieved in the coming year and what needs to be achieved to meet goals highlights the problems that have to be solved. The annual budget is part of the planning process for meeting strategic objectives.

British Airways describes the function and importance of the annual budget in its Annual Report. 'A three year business plan sets the business agenda. The plan communicates the corporate strategy, agrees targets for financial returns and service standards, identifies and prioritises improvement opportunities to deliver the targets and agrees capital and manpower requirements. The business plan priorities link into the annual budgeting process which defines specific departmental action plans.'

There is general dissatisfaction with the budgeting process; it takes too long (average 4.5 months) and too much effort. There is no doubt that targets and forecasts are essential and are helpful for guiding a company, but there is a search for a 'better way'; watch this space.

In smaller companies often too little time is spent setting targets or budgets and comparing actual performance against them. A survey reported in the magazine *Financial Management* showed:

Document	Percentage of small companies that: Budget	Compare with actual budget
Profit and Loss Account	60%	40%
Balance Sheet	60%	35%
Cash Flow	80%	40%
Bank Balance	95%	40%

Preparation of the key targets need not be a time-consuming process, even in a small company. Simple computer software is available to help small businesses. Regardless of the size of the company, directors should agree targets and monitor performance against them.

CHAIRMAN'S STATEMENT

Before the Annual Report to Shareholders is prepared, directors should agree with the chairman the matters that should be included in the Chairman's Report and Operating Review. The Board should not be in the position of merely agreeing a final draft prepared by others. The Chairman's Report and Operating Review are vital communication documents; for some companies they are their only communication with the world outside the company! The documents should contain a balanced view of what is going on in the company, put into the context of what is happening in the industry. An honest company will discuss its concerns as well as its achievements. Some reports paint a favourable picture of the company's position, avoiding discussion of areas of worry.

In most countries there are annual awards for the best company Annual Reports (you may wonder why there is not a list of the worst, people learn more from failures than successes). These Annual Reports will be a good guide to the standard of communication all companies should aim for. It is also useful to look at the Annual Reports that win awards in other countries.

The Commonwealth Association for Corporate Governance has a model Annual Report on its website (see Useful Contacts, p 182).

THE CHAIRMAN'S ROLE

The chairman plays the key role in leading the team, the Board of Directors. The chairman has a number of special functions which can best be carried out if the chairman is non-executive, hence not involved in day-to-day decisions.

The chairman:

- leads the Board

- should periodically review the composition and performance of the Board, taking advice from all other directors (the needs of the company change over time)

- needs a clear view on the priority of issues needing resolution

- approves the agenda for Board meetings

- is responsible for ensuring that each director receives the information they need to function as a Board member

- must ensure that there is a clear definition of the Board's powers, role and responsibilities, that all directors agree them and that they are recorded; and ensure that the responsibilities and powers delegated to individual directors or groups of directors are clear, meet the current needs of the company and follow the current best practice of corporate governance

- tends to be the company's leading representative to the public and may be expected to speak to the press and discuss with stakeholders aspects of the company and its future

- runs the formal meetings of shareholders, the Annual General Meeting and any Extraordinary General Meetings

- plays a leading role in recommending the composition of Board committees

- leads the Board evaluation process

- should be a leader in the widest of senses.

During the Board meeting and discussion of reports and issues, the chairman's job is to stimulate a frank exchange of views, to draw out those who are silent and to make silent the verbose and voluble. All directors should contribute to discussion and debate, for after all, if a director does not add substance to the debate, what are they doing on the Board?

KEY POINT

The chairman needs to aid discussion, to be a facilitator not a dominator.

A particular responsibility for the chairman is to ensure that all differences of opinions are drawn into the open. Each director is on the board to help achieve the success of the company; all are on the same side. The exploration of issues and all concerns openly can only make the decision better.

> At one Board meeting I was, apparently, the only director against a recommended course of action. After recording my views, the decision was made to follow the recommendation. I learnt after the meeting that some other directors were also against the proposal, but preferred to argue against it 'covertly'. Not my idea of the job of a director!

There will inevitably be disagreements and differences of opinion between Board members, and these need to be respected. The chairman should create an atmosphere in which all directors can be open in the discussions. All discussions are directed towards co-operation and respect.

ACCURATE INFORMATION

Directors are entitled to assume that the information they are given before or at a Board meeting is accurate. This does not mean unquestioning acceptance of everything that is said or written! Sensible judgement, a director's 'stock in trade', must be used. In order to help the process, directors need to be satisfied that the company has internal control procedures in place and that the process of producing information is reliable. This will give the directors the confidence to use the information. Identifying minor typing errors in reports is, however, not constructive and is irritating to colleagues.

An active internal audit function, or if the company does not have its own department, a periodic review by the company's external auditors, of the procedures that generate information for the Board, should be sufficient to give directors some comfort. The annual ritual witch-hunt to reduce the audit fee can be counter-productive in the long run. The audit function should be seen as an aid to the company's management.

MONITORING

One of the Board's functions is to monitor the current performance of the company. This can lead to a split in the Board; it is easier for non-executive directors and independent non-executive directors to take a detached view of performance than executive directors. Unless this area is handled well, the non-executives will become a 'Panel of Critics' of the executive directors. The non-executive directors are not the shareholders' watchdogs, but are equal members of the company's guiding team; both executive and non-executives directors need to keep this in mind. The chairman plays an important part in ensuring that the monitoring role is handled well. All directors need to be aware of the trap of permitting a Board to split into groups or 'camps'.

A particularly interesting role for the non-executive directors is to keep the executive directors focussed on achieving the objectives already set. Change in an organisation generally does not happen quickly. Making a decision and announcing it is not the same as achieving the change. If the change is to company structure or management attitude or priorities, it can take a generation of managers before the change is fully embedded in the organisation. There is a temptation for directors to assume that, after a period, the planned changes have been made, while in truth the organisation has only just started to understand what is really needed and involved.

Directors should not forget that everyone is in favour of change provided that it does not mean they have to do anything differently!

> There was a classic comment in one letter I received, 'We welcome innovation, provided it does not mean change.' I think it was meant to be a joke, but you never know!

The company needs to remain focussed on achieving its objectives even if this takes years. The non-executive directors can play an important role in this.

CONFLICT OF INTEREST AT THE BOARD MEETING

Each director will have registered any potential conflict of interest and regularly informed the Board of any changes (see discussion on page 33). Despite this vigilance, it is advisable, if an agenda item involves a conflict of interest, for a director to remind colleagues of the conflict before discussions start. A conflict of interest is an active issue, not a bureaucratic formality.

If a director does have a conflict in a particular matter, they should not speak on the subject nor vote on the related recommendation or decision. In serious circumstances the director should withdraw from the Board meeting while the matter is being discussed. Serious circumstances might be where a director has a connection with an organisation planning to compete with the company for business.

> A director representing a shareholder in a five-way joint venture company announced that the shareholder would join another consortium to bid against the company for a particular project. The director not only withdrew from the discussions of the bid, but also did not receive any of the papers relating to the company's offer and received only an edited copy of the minutes of the meeting. It might be argued that the director should have resigned from the Board, but that would have meant that a significant shareholder was not represented on the Board. Careful handling was needed.

If the director with a conflict of interests does stay in the meeting during discussion of the item, they must treat all information and comments as strictly confidential.

Disagreement over conflict of interest is a difficult area. Should a director, who thinks another director has a conflict of interests and does not raise the issue, have any liability?

DURING THE MEETING

Directors at the meeting should aim to contribute to discussions, speaking clearly and concisely. If the Board is working well, with a good agenda, all major reports and proposals circulated before the meeting and a point of contact for clarifying queries before the meeting, the discussions should be well focussed. Directors should not be frightened to ask questions; similarly they should not be afraid to sit and listen to what others have to say. Directors should say what they believe and believe what they say.

'Good' questions are those directed at real issues:

'If we really value our staff, why is our staff resignation rate higher than the average for the industry?'

'If we are customer focussed, why do we have a low re-purchase rate?'

Board discussions need to be orderly. Questions and comments should be directed to the chairman. At the end of the each discussion the chairman should summarise the exchanges and state what action has been agreed. Some Boards are formal and everyone is addressed by their surname, others use first names. The form does not matter or change the need for an orderly discussion with comments directed via the chairman.

The Board's responsibility for monitoring operations and progress towards achieving agreed goals means, generally, the Board receive reports from executive directors. Where possible these reports should be circulated to all directors before the meeting so there is the chance to read the report and clarify any issues.

I have attended Board meetings where executive directors were permitted to read out typed reports on the operation of

their function. This took 75 per cent of the meeting, leaving almost no time to consider the information and little time for discussion (perhaps the object of the exercise!). Reading out reports which could be circulated to directors before the meeting is a waste of the Board's time.

It is important that all directors, of whatever classification, have the knowledge to ask questions at the Board meeting and are happy to do so. Minor questions and requests for clarification should have been dealt with before the meeting, when the papers were received, through discussion with the company's designated contact point. The door always remains open to ask further questions and to question issues arising from discussions at the Board meeting.

Disagreement and conflict

During discussions directors should express their views either agreeing or disagreeing with others in line with their own opinion. All directors are on the same side – the company's. Seeking conflict or being controversial or unco-operative for the sake of it does not help the process. 'Independent' is defined as not being dependent on another person for one's livelihood or opinions; it does not mean being arrogant or difficult.

While directors must say what they think, a director cannot forever be at variance with everyone else on the Board on every issue; otherwise the Board will not operate as a team. In the rare circumstances that a director becomes a constant thorn in the side of the Board, then in fairness to the other members of the Board and the future of the company, they should resign. The chairman may need to take a lead in arranging this.

'Profit is the reward for risk.'

All decision-making involves risk. While directors need to understand the potential benefits of each course of action and weigh them against the risks, the existence of risk should not mean that an action is not taken. All directors need to understand the threats to a company and the opportunities that exist. Co-operation between executive and non-executive directors is important in this area. Directors may have different views of risks and opportunities and these need to be brought together in order to balance the decision.

Summary and decision making
After directors have discussed an issue at the board meeting, the chairman will:

◆ summarise the discussions
◆ describe the recommendation or decision reached
◆ articulate the action agreed.

To be fully effective the action agreed should also describe the expected outcome or result of the decision, often called a **success measure**. Achieving or failing to reach the success measure tells the Board whether the objective – e.g. increased market share by a certain date – has been reached. Measurement and management sit closely together.

The chairman summarises the discussions for the benefit of not only the directors but also the record keeper (minute taker, perhaps the company secretary), also stating clearly the decision or recommendation of the Board. This is a crucial point in the meeting, because the decision or recommendation will be recorded in the company's minute book (minuted) and unless challenged will become part of the company's official record. If a director does not agree with the decision or recommendation their dissenting opinion should be noted in the minutes. If the decision is still carried despite the opposing view, the director must accept the decision and support it.

At most Board meetings decisions will be made by consensus or a simple majority vote, unless the company's Article of Association say otherwise. Frequently in joint-venture companies or where there is a majority shareholder, the simple 51% rule will not apply. Directors will be aware of the rules from the due diligence process. In any event the company secretary will be aware of all special rules or requirements.

Communication of outcomes

The Board's focus on 'where are we going' means that the Board should keep a good and open relationship with shareholders and all the company's stakeholders. There is little point in developing and agreeing a strategy, if that strategy is not explained to staff and suppliers. Staff will, after all, be charged with delivering the performance. Major sub-contractors or service suppliers need to know what part they have to play in the company's future. Achieving strategic goals requires the co-ordinated action of many.

KEY POINT

Communication, motivation and clarity achieve strategic goals.

STAKEHOLDERS' INTERESTS

The Board needs to be clear who the company's stakeholders are and what they need in terms of information or resources, to help the company. Stakeholders are not identical; each has different needs, and each will play a different role in achieving success.

The broad categories of stakeholders are:

- shareholders
- employees
- customers
- suppliers
- community and government.

It is frequently advised that the discussions by the Board must take into account the 'legitimate interests of stakeholders'. The legitimate interests of stakeholders other than shareholders are difficult to pin down, changing with public opinion and circumstances. The 'legitimate' i.e. 'lawful' interests are not defined in law, so what are they? There is no full answer. Institutes of directors give some guidance, but this area is still developing and seeking definition.

This difficulty does not absolve directors from considering the effect of their decisions on those connected to the company. Directors need to be sensitive to the views and positions of stakeholders and hold them in mind during discussions. It may be that some stakeholders' desires cannot be met and the only course of action may be to explain the position and the reasons for the decision to that class of stakeholder. This may not make everyone happy, but at least everyone is clear that the company did consider all views and attempted to include them in the final decision.

All members of the Board should be able and prepared to speak to groups of stakeholders either at group meetings or individually, if requested by the chairman. There may be times when a particular director's words will be more convincing (see the example below).

COMMUNICATION WITH STAKEHOLDERS

A very important responsibility of the Board is communication. Communication is the joint responsibility of all directors. This does not mean that each member of the Board needs to speak to each employee, banker or supplier, but the Board should jointly decide what needs to be communicated to each group of stakeholders and who will be responsible for the making the communication. Non-executive directors are not excluded from the process and can be a very helpful voice.

> **An investor bought a significant but not majority shareholding in another public company and appointed some of its executive directors as non-executive directors on the Board. When the transaction was announced to the company's staff, one of the new non-executive directors attended the meeting and answered questions about the investor's ideas and attitude to the company. This job could only be done convincingly by the investor's representative and it was well received by the staff.**

The 'what' and 'how' of the information that needs to be communicated is a continuing debate. The Higgs report noted that in the UK, 'individual share ownership has fallen from over 50% of the market in the 1960s to less than one fifth today' (2003). The *Economist* in April 2003 noted that 'institutional investors own a bigger share of American equities than ever before: 49%, four times as much as 40 years ago.'

Institutional investors generally want more information, more quickly. The Internet allows information and formal reports to be circulated quickly and for anyone to question a company's Board and management. However, Boards question whether more information is necessarily better.

In 2002 Coca Cola decided not to follow the trend of publishing more information each quarter and stopped giving quarterly and annual earnings estimates, but undertook to give more information on progress towards achieving long-term goals.

Having communicated with the organisation and stakeholders on where the company is going and what needs to be achieved, the Board is responsible for ensuring that the resources, staff with the right skills, funds, equipment and training are available to meet those needs. After that the Board must monitor progress.

It all sounds very simple, but it is not. It is a hard process. It is managing this difficult process and achieving success that produces the job satisfaction for a director.

DISTRIBUTING DIVIDENDS
The Board also recommends dividends. In some cases there are legal

limits on the amounts which can be distributed, e.g. dividends can only be paid out of realised profits (those profits which are certain and received). There may be special limits for public companies. Specialist companies such as banks or insurance companies may have more specific requirements.

Loan documents frequently set maximum limits for the amount of dividend, either directly through a stated ratio or indirectly by setting a maximum for the 'Quick Ratio' (Current Assets/Current Liabilities, see page 113).

Each director should have become aware of these limitations during their due diligence review.

CONTINGENCY PLANS

It is prudent for the Board to have contingency plans for unusual, but possible events, e.g. what to do in the event of receiving a take-over bid or in a major crisis such as a product failure or a major accident. These are not matters solely for executive directors; the full Board should agree the contingency plans for major happenings. Generally, implementation of the plans will be in the hands of the executive directors, but in some circumstances non-executives directors may be required to help, for example the chairman speaking to staff to explain what has happened and what action is being taken, or directors meeting the staff handling the problem.

In the event of insolvency or suspected insolvency, the responsibilities of the Board change to one of focussing on protecting the interest of the creditors. It may well be that specialist advisors will be needed to help the Board do this well.

SUMMARY

To participate well at a Board meeting a director should:

◆ consider the issues to be decided impartially and objectively

◆ be positive about potential strategies

◆ address issues, not personalities

◆ stay focussed on agenda items

◆ offer constructive analysis, not criticism

◆ insist on being fully informed

◆ make points briefly and concisely

◆ support the chairman.

A good non-executive director will:

◆ have the key skills to
  − identify gaps in a plan or proposal
  − motivate management
  − prevent complacency

◆ raise issues, not confront executives

◆ be a sounding board for the executives responsible for implementing policy

◆ work to avoid executive directors closing ranks against them

◆ work in partnership with executives who share the same approach to a project.

7

Action After the Board Meeting

What should a director do after the Board meeting? A director is a director every day, not just at Board meetings. There are things to be done by both executive and non-executive directors.

DIFFERENCES OF OPINION

During directors' meetings opinions should be expressed openly and frankly. Discussion can be lively and spirited, with the chairman acting as referee. If there is a dissenting view which cannot be reconciled to the position of the majority and to the final decision of the Board, the right course is for the minutes to record the director's observations and reservation so they become part of the company's records. The Board's decision will still stand.

CABINET RESPONSIBILITY

Once outside the meeting, all directors should accept and support the decision reached, this is **cabinet responsibility**. Just as independence is a state of mind and difficult to define, so is cabinet responsibility, the recommended behaviour of directors after a meeting.

Ex-Prime Minister of the UK, Margaret Thatcher's explanation of the term is, 'You thrash things out in private and you agree publicly to defend the collective decision. . . If you don't . . . there's no reason for having cabinet government [a Board of Directors]. You might just as well have a Prime Minister [Chief Executive Officer] saying, 'This is what we're going to do.'

In any discussion with third parties, particularly the company's staff, emphasis should be on the validity of the decision, not the differences of opinion expressed before arriving at it. This does not mean that a director should lie, simply that any discussion of the decision should avoid detailing the various differences of opinion. Unity increases the chances that the decision will achieve its objective.

When a decision has been made, the emphasis is to make it work. Any questions about whether or not there were dissenting views should be dealt with in a general way, concluding that following an exchange of views the decision was made and is supported by all directors. No amount of analysis, calculation of 'downsides' (risks) and 'upsides' (benefits) or numbers of scenarios will guarantee that a decision will be right. Being in the majority does not make a director right nor does being in a minority make a director wrong.

KEY POINT

Each Board decision should be supported whole-heartedly by all directors to help the company achieve the objective; anything other than unity will be destructive.

Extreme circumstances
There will, on rare occasions, be decisions of such importance from a business or ethical standpoint that the cabinet responsibility approach is just not a workable option. There may be some decisions where views are so divided, opinions so strongly held and the decision so important that the dissenting director believes that just having the opposing view minuted is not enough. In these circumstances the only course for a director is to resign from the Board. This would be in very extreme circumstances.

If this happens in a public company, a press announcement will probably have to be made, to meet Stock Exchange regulations and the genuine need and right of shareholders to know what is going on. It is unlikely that the average director will ever meet this situation and it is not something to be feared, but every director has to be prepared to back their opinion with the appropriate level of action. For the vast majority of decisions all that is needed is for a director to sincerely express their views and then to be part of the united front supporting a decision.

If a difficult or potentially contentious issue is scheduled for discussion at a Board meeting, each director should make every effort to attend the meeting. Failure to take part in the discussion and resolution of a difficult issue would be considered as negligence in some jurisdictions.

Dealing with doubts

No director is infallible, nor are they expected to be. There are too many examples of company Boards being right for the wrong reasons as well as wrong for the wrong reasons.

Should there be any doubt in your mind about supporting a Board decision, the first person to discuss the problem with is the chairman of the Board. If this discussion does not put your mind at rest then a talk with the company's legal advisor, with or without the chairman present, will probably resolve the matter one way or the other.

CONFIDENTIAL INFORMATION

A director leaves the Board meeting with a considerable amount of confidential information, partly written and partly in their memory, from the discussion of problems and opportunities. You are responsible for keeping all of this information completely confidential. The information, if released to a third party, could be damaging to the company; hence it is better never to discuss the confidential affairs of the company with anyone, even in an informal discussion with a fellow director, in a public place. Conversations can be overheard. Care is needed.

I have on more than one occasion, on an aircraft, overheard two directors reviewing a Board's discussion of quite confidential issues. Those sitting in the seats around them could clearly hear the conversation.

Directors are, individually and collectively, responsible for ensuring that all information is kept confidential. This becomes particularly important if there is a major deal brewing. Being 'responsible' means knowing what procedures are in place to ensure confidentiality, within the company, amongst the company's advisors and within the Board, and being satisfied that they are adequate and working.

If it is a publicly quoted company and the directors are not confident that the system is secure or if confidentiality has been breached, the Stock Exchange's Listing Rules will include some procedure for informing the public. This will probably be some form of paid announcement in the major newspapers to advise shareholders and potential investors of the current situation.

If one company is negotiating to buy another and this accidentally slips out at a meeting with the press on another subject, frequently the Stock Exchange will require that the Board on behalf of the company put a paid advertisement describing the deal in the major newspapers for the next day. The advertisement will probably be required to describe the potential deal and confirm that negotiations are continuing, but that no agreement has been reached and that an agreement may not be reached.

This type of 'finger in the dyke' announcement is a last resort and it would be very much better for everyone if the discussions were to remain confidential until a clear conclusion is reached.

There is no point becoming paranoid about confidentiality, but there is no doubt that care is needed. 'Just because you are paranoid, doesn't mean THEY aren't listening!'

ACTION AFTER THE MEETING

Executive Directors
The executive directors will get on with their job of running the daily business of the company and seeking to achieve the goals set by the Board, within the policies agreed by the Board.

A non-executive director or independent non-executive director can leave the meeting knowing that the management team will work diligently to achieve what has been agreed. Having been part of the process of establishing the goals and policies, the executive directors will ensure the organisation will work within the framework and policies the Board has established.

Non-executive directors

To some extent the non-executives can leave the meeting with a lighter heart than the executive directors, but there is still work to do. They must continue to keep up to date with developments in the economy and industry that could affect the future of the company; policies and strategies may have to be reviewed if there are unexpected significant changes in circumstances. A new director, whether executive or non-executive, should continue with their plan of familiarisation visits to major operating locations.

If there are dramatic changes in the economy, in the industry or in the fortunes of a major competitor, a non-executive director may wish to contact the chairman to discuss whether the matter needs to be on the agenda for the next Board meeting. If an urgent debate is needed, a special Board meeting to discuss the issue and its effects on the company will be very useful and helpful.

Emergency Board meetings

Although in most circumstances the regular schedule of Board meetings should be sufficient to deal with the direction of the company, there are circumstances when the Board will need to meet more frequently. There is always the facility to call an emergency meeting of directors. If it is necessary to have an emergency meeting the chairman and company secretary should use their best efforts to send all directors an outline, however brief, of the situation before the meeting. If the urgency is such that this just can't be done, there should be a detailed presentation with an analysis of the situation and the potential effects on the company at the beginning of the Board meeting before the discussion starts.

DECISIONS OUTSIDE A MEETING

A director, whether, non-executive or executive, may be asked to make a decision between scheduled Board meetings. The Articles of Association of most companies permit **resolutions** (decisions) **in circulation**. This method can be used when the company, at the prompting of the chairman or an executive director, requires a Board decision to be made before the next Board meeting, but the matter does not warrant a special meeting of directors. The chairman or executive director must prepare a detailed written Board paper with details of:

♦ the reason why the decision is needed outside a Board Meeting
♦ a description of the background to the decision
♦ expected benefits
♦ how and when the benefits or result will appear
♦ risks to the company
♦ how the risks will be managed
♦ how success or failure will be measured.

The end of the Board paper will include a written resolution, which the director must consider. The Board paper should be reviewed and signed by the chairman before it is circulated to each director. It is good form, and sensible, for the executive director requesting the decision to sign the Board paper before it is sent to other directors.

Each director should read the detailed proposal and, if persuaded, sign, agreeing to the resolution. If there are any questions on the proposal these should be directed to the chairman to answer. If the answers not persuasive, the matter should be discussed with the chairman; the options are the same as voting at a Board meeting.

The company secretary will usually be responsible for arranging the circulation to all directors.

This is a very useful device for handling routine matters between Board meetings as it provides a detailed record of the proposal and the resolution. It also provides a useful way to keep the business operating without calling frequent Board meetings, particularly if directors are in different locations.

The disadvantage is that the chance of a full discussion and exchange of views on the proposal is lost.

Resolutions in Circulation should be restricted to matters that are not controversial, e.g. approval of the details of a bank borrowing that has already been agreed in outline at a previous Board meeting and authorising a named person to sign the agreements with the bank.

The resolution will become effective when the last director signs approving the resolution. The rules for the procedure will be detailed in the company's Articles of Association.

To avoid any confusion and to permit directors to discuss the Resolution in Circulation if they wish, each Board paper circulated should be presented to the next Board meeting and confirmed by the directors.

Paper Board meetings
There can be circumstances, e.g. when Resolutions in Circulation are not permitted in a jurisdiction, when a company will hold a

paper Board meeting. This may seem to be a useful procedure, but it is not recommended and if used must be very carefully and closely controlled.

For a paper meeting, minutes of a Board meeting are prepared as if the meeting had been held and all directors attended, but the directors do not actually attend. The danger is obvious.

The circumstances when this method can be considered are limited to those where only a few absolutely routine matters need a resolution, e.g. authorising the company secretary to arrange and call the Annual General Meeting – and when directors are in different locations. Each director must be contacted before the date of the paper meeting, advised of the matter that is proposed to be dealt with 'on paper' and their agreement gained to the method and the matter to be decided. The company secretary will prepare minutes for the paper meeting as if it had taken place and these will be approved at the next meeting of directors.

Paper meetings are not a recommended way of dealing with Board matters, but the approach is sometimes used, so you need to be aware of the process. If this approach is used frequently, directors must consider whether the annual work plan for the Board needs to be amended to avoid paper meetings.

There is a sub-set of the paper meeting. If the company's Articles of Association permit directors to attend meetings electronically, a conference call involving all directors can be considered a 'meeting'. For this approach to be effective, directors should receive a detailed Board paper before the telephone call.

TRADING WHILE INSOLVENT

If the company is in danger of trading while insolvent or is actually insolvent, directors cannot forget about the problem between Board meetings. Executive directors will be dealing with the difficulties every day, but non-executive directors have a responsibility to stay in touch and to be available to give advice.

Any unexpected deterioration or improvement in the company's position should be advised to directors. Not only do directors need to be kept in the picture, but they also need to be able to respond to changes. An urgent Board meeting may be needed or perhaps a formal re-assessment of the company's position.

'Hovering round' insolvency is a difficult and stressful time for all directors. Care and a clear head are needed.

If the company's forecast balance sheet and long-term cash forecast indicate that it could have funding problems akin to insolvency, the Board should immediately establish to its satisfaction whether the forecast position is indeed valid. If it is, the Board can consider appointing an independent adviser to examine the current and forecast financial position. It can be difficult for the Board and management to view a potential insolvent position independently and the help of an adviser can very useful. It is better to initiate this work before insolvency actually occurs.

What might happen

Although a creditor's first priority will be to protect its position, usually creditors, including banks, prefer to help a company overcome its financial difficulties than to seek the liquidation of the company. Debenture holders can appoint a **Receiver**, who is a person authorised to manage the affairs of insolvent companies. Frequently the debenture holders will refrain from acting if the company is already taking positive action to resolve the problem, particularly if the problem is forecast to be a temporary fund shortfall.

There are many solutions to a funding problem, ranging from re-scheduling liabilities through sale and lease back arrangements to a complete re-financing. In serious cases the company may have to appoint an administrator or receiver or propose a **Scheme of Arrangement** (a reconstruction of the business).

KEY POINT

When facing a possible insolvency there is a lot for directors to learn in a short time. It will be important that all directors stay in touch with the situation as it develops and co-operate to reach a sensible solution.

The Board's responsibility

The Board's responsibility if insolvency is looming is to ensure the position of creditors is protected. The company takes second place. Insolvency, like love, changes everything!

Valid forecasts, questioning assumptions and vigilance are strong protections against insolvency. Trading profitably is the best defence!

CONTINUING YOUR EDUCATION

Between Board meetings each director should continue their education in directorship and the company's operations. There are plenty of courses that will extend a director's knowledge.

The best approach is to prepare a plan which co-ordinates any courses with the director's education about the workings of the company. A course on marketing could be very useful before a visit to the company's marketing and sales department.

Before starting on a programme of learning it should be established who will pay the course fee. Some companies will pay the bill. A helpful approach can be for each director to be allocated an amount annually that can be spent on their own training in 'directorship', provided all training is approved in advance by the chairman.

> In Malaysia, directors are required to:
> ◆ attend 1.5 days of formal training
> ◆ have continuing training each year.
>
> This requirement for 'continuing training' follows the practice established in other professions, e.g. accountancy.

It may be more difficult for executive directors to find the time to attend courses on directorship or to be briefed on the operations of other parts of the company's operations, but time must be found if the director is to do a good job. A director's job is essential and it deserves to be done well – a lot hangs on the Board's decisions.

SUMMARY

What a Director should do between Board meetings:

◆ Support the decisions made.

◆ **Executive directors**
  – Run the business.

      – Make progress towards achieving the company's strategic goal.

      – Work within the policies and guidelines agreed by the Board.

♦ **Non-executive directors**

      – Stay informed about company events, the industry and economy.

      – Be available to advise the chairman.

      – Offer comments to the chairman on important developments.

      – Keep up to date with sub-committee work.

♦ Continue familiarisation with the company.

♦ Continue with an education programme in 'directorship'.

♦ **If insolvency is a worry**

      – Look at forecasts of the financial position.

      – Get advice.

      – Stay in touch with the chairman.

8

Leaving the Board

Once you have has settled into the Board, know the working of the company well, understand the responsibilities, work well with the other directors and may even be receiving some reasonable fees, why would you ever want to leave?

WHEN TO LEAVE A BOARD

There are three broad reasons for leaving a Board:

- when the time comes to retire
- when you are required to leave the Board
- when you want to resign from the Board.

RETIREMENT

What is the local recommendation? Although the UK, Australia, New Zealand and Hong Kong do not have a mandatory retirement age for directors, each country deals with a director's age in a different way.

In Australia the law requires that after the age of 72 years a director should be re-elected each year regardless of the usual period of appointment for younger directors. In New Zealand it is recommended that the Board regularly review the risks attendant upon age and long service of directors. The Hong Kong Institute of Directors recommends that directors, of whatever age, are appointed for only one or two years and that the Board must decide whether a director is adding value. The Higgs Report puts forward the idea that a non-executive director could serve two terms of three years, with further terms being subject to shareholders' approval.

It seems strange that in an era of improving health and extended life expectancy, 'best practice' should recommend that a director consider retiring at what can be a young age. It may be that part of the logic is that it is sometimes difficult to persuade a long-serving director to retire once deteriorating health starts to impair performance. It could be the fear that in a rapidly changing world older directors might be reluctant to accept positive changes. The performance of a director will always depend on the individual. The chairman of the Board must assess each director's performance regularly and regardless of their age in years decide whether their continued appointment benefits the company.

Directors should attend and participate in a majority of Board meetings, not just a minimum of 50 per cent. In some jurisdictions, e.g. Malaysia, there is a requirement that directors attend more than half the meetings in a year; if this is not done, the director must retire.

The benefits of age and experience

Experience is a useful and valuable asset, particularly to a company in a cyclical industry. Directors with short experience on the Board may not have seen the reactions, problems and opportunities that arise during a 'boom' and a 'bust'. History does not repeat itself exactly, but history and experience teach valuable lessons. Directors should have a few business 'scars'. The economic cycle is alive and well and waiting to catch the unwary. A few 'grey hairs' on the Board can help during difficult times, whether the difficulties arise from rapid expansion or a slump in business.

It is sad for a company to lose the useful experience an individual has accumulated during their career as a director, but at some stage each director must move on.

WHEN A DIRECTOR IS REQUIRED TO LEAVE

The second circumstance is a little more difficult. When should a director leave the Board?

The most obvious time for an executive director is when accepting a job with a competitor. Clearly there would be a considerable conflict of interest if the director tried to remain on both boards. But what if an executive director joins a company that is not in competition? There is a debate about whether there is an advantage to the company if the director stays on the board as a non-executive director. On the one hand there is the value of keeping the experience of the company and industry and adding the new experience of another industry. On the other hand there is the possibility that their successor as executive director may be intimidated by the presence of the predecessor on the Board. If the company does wish to keep the executive director on the Board, it is necessary to discuss the time commitment with the new employer.

Despite the debate, generally when an executive director decides to join even a non-competing company, they will resign from the Board, if only so that they can devote all their efforts to the new position. This is the approach advocated by some experts in corporate governance.

Some countries suggest that executive directors be appointed for specific periods. The New Zealand Stock Exchange recommends that an executive director should not stay in office for more than five years without being re-appointed by the shareholders.

It can be argued that there is a net benefit in a retiring executive director staying on the Board as a non-executive director. The arguments are similar to those for an executive director joining another company; the benefits of keeping the detailed knowledge of the business and industry against potentially inhibiting the performance of the successor. The latter can become a real problem if the successor plans to substantially change some of the practices or policies introduced by the predecessor.

As with so many problems in corporate governance the answer to the dilemma is an emphatic, 'Well, it all depends.' People will always be people, and the right course is likely to be determined by the chairman based on the personality of the retiring director and the successor. Judgement on the pros and cons will probably be made by the chairman advised by the non-executive directors and the Nomination Committee.

In one public company there has been a tradition of the retiring chairman staying on the Board as a non-executive director, not attending every Board meeting, but attending the majority. This approach seems to have worked well, perhaps because of the good working relationships amongst all directors. None of the executive directors have, to the best of my recollection, stayed on as a non-executive director.

Perhaps the lesson from the example above is that a chairman with wide business experience can continue to contribute without inhibiting the successor. The other executive directors should move over and give their successors a clear run at the job without casting any 'long shadows' over the Board table. Circumstances and personalities will determine which will be the best course for the company.

Failure to meet goals

There is the question of whether all or some of the directors, executive and/or non-executive, should resign if the company fails to meet its agreed goals. There is a strong argument that failure should not be rewarded by continued employment. Those directors associated with the failure should move on and leave the way clear to others to improve the position. On the other hand it can be argued strongly that those responsible for failure should not be allowed to walk away, but should be responsible for correcting the situation. The debate continues. The right course is the one that is seen as being the best for the company by the shareholders at a general meeting. The shareholders have the right to remove one, some or all directors.

The same logic applies to a specific problem, which features frequently in the press. If it becomes clear that the company's executives have an 'excessive' remuneration package, should the members of the company's Remuneration Committee offer their resignations to the shareholders? There is no clear answer.

Removal by shareholders

A director can be removed from the Board by the shareholders. In most jurisdictions this action will require approval of a special resolution at an Extraordinary General Meeting of Shareholders.

There will be some notice period, often 21 days, and a copy of the notice calling the meeting will be sent by the company secretary to the director involved, so any attempt to remove a director will not be a surprise. The director has the chance to speak to the meeting or to write to the shareholders to rebut any accusation or to explain their actions. Shareholders do not often remove a director, but every director needs to be aware of the potential.

Disqualification

There are times when a director is required to retire and leave the Board; these will be listed in the company's Articles of Association and probably company law. Typical circumstances are:

◆ becoming bankrupt
◆ being adjudged of unsound mind.

Where a country has a requirement that a director attend a minimum number of meetings, failure to do so means the director should resign.

A director may become disqualified from becoming or remaining a director for a number of other reasons. The list will also be found in the company's Articles of Association and in company law. The list of offences constitute failure to act correctly as a director and include:

◆ fraud
◆ persistently failing to submit Annual Returns
◆ not acting in a prudent manner, if the company becomes insolvent.

The list is really common sense.

CHOOSING TO RESIGN FROM THE BOARD

We live in a free world and a director can retire whenever they believe the time is right. Ill health or the demands of other commitments are obvious reasons why a director may want to resign. As in all cases, the over-riding consideration is what will be in the best interests of the company.

Lack of time – or motivation

The Board of Directors is an organisational tool through which a company achieves its objectives and that 'tool' has to be sharp and effective all of the time. It is quite possible that a non-executive director has become bored and no longer interested in dealing with the affairs of a company or industry and does not feel motivated to continue. It may be that, following an excellent performance on one Board, the director has been approached to join other Boards and there is simply not sufficient time to spend on the affairs of each company. Directors need to have sufficient time, not only to study Board reports and think about the implications, but also to attend possibly extended Board meetings.

> I have seen cases where a director, a busy businessman, has allocated two hours for a Board meeting and left the meeting after two hours for another appointment, even though there were still major agenda items to be discussed.

The director described above is not fulfilling his important role in the company. If leaving a Board meeting early becomes a regular occurrence, others might even take advantage of his short attention span and leave contentious items to the later part of the meeting when fewer directors are present.

If a director runs out of time and has to leave a meeting, perhaps the chairman had failed to control the meeting or assess how much time was needed to fully discuss each agenda item. On the other hand, the director may have too many responsibilities. Whatever the reason, directors need to be available for all agenda items. It may make a non-executive director feel important to be rushing from one Board meeting to another, but they must question whether they are really doing their job with the depth of concentration the responsibilities really deserve.

In some jurisdictions there is a recommendation for the maximum number of directorships one individual should hold; five is a number frequently quoted. The number which can be comfortably handled will depend on the demands of each company.

When a director's skills are no longer needed

An individual director may believe they are no longer contributing constructively to the discussions at the Board meeting. This concern should be discussed with the chairman. The chairman of the Board is the leader of the team and responsible for dealing with the performance and worries of individual directors.

The needs and priorities of a company do change over time. When the major focus of the company is, say, building a new factory or developing a new distribution network, certain skills will predominate on a Board. During more stable times a different range of skills will be needed and perhaps the composition of the Board should be changed. This logic applies not only to non-executive directors, but also to executive directors. Matching the skills on the Board with the needs of the company usually falls to the chairman, with the advice of the chief executive officer and the Nomination

Committee if one exists. No director should have a 'job for life', even if they represent a major shareholder!

An ideal time to discuss this type of matter is during the chairman's regular meeting with each director to discuss:

◆ their contribution to the Board's discussions
◆ the overall performance of the Board
◆ any worries a director has.

BOARD ASSESSMENT

Some directors will be shocked to hear that their individual performance as a director needs to be assessed together with the overall effectiveness of the Board, but that is what should happen. The Institute of Directors of New Zealand lists as one of the duties of the Chairman:

> *Monitoring and evaluating the individual performance of directors and taking the initiative in instigating periodic evaluations of the Board as a whole.*

There is similar wording in the 'Guidelines for Boards and Directors' issued by the Commonwealth Association for Corporate Governance. The UK's Institute of Directors, in its 'Good Practice for Directors, Standards for the Board', includes under 'Board Management':

> *Appraising...evaluates the performance of the Board and its members and provides appropriate feedback.*

To keep the balance right, the other members of the Board need to assess the performance of the chairman and the chief executive officer; everyone should go through the same review process.

In reality most directors, whether executive or non-executive, should not feel threatened by a regular performance review. After all, many of them will have been through the same process while working in an organisation. It is interesting to speculate how many Boards review directors' performance with the same dedication and rigour as the annual review of staff performance.

There is nothing difficult in organising the review of directors' performance and contribution; it is simply a matter of discussing a list of items. Most institutes of directors produce some form of checklist of the items to be discussed; some even have an electronic system that can be used. The aim is to make sure that the leadership of a company is working well. It does, however, also provide an opportunity to review what skills the company needs to have at its disposal on the Board and where those skills are to be found.

The assessment can take place in whatever form directors feel most comfortable with, either:

◆ a face-to-face talk, with the chairman speaking to an individual director

◆ in a group discussion

◆ by completing a questionnaire with a checklist of items to be assessed.

The annual review also gives a director and chairman a chance to discuss any matters that worry either of them. The Board is a team and all need to be able to speak freely. The discussion should be two-way, real communication; it is a chance for each director to express their views on how the Board is working. The process is easy to arrange in any size of company.

There could be a problem if a non-executive director or an executive director has been nominated to the Board by a major shareholder. The chairman still has the same responsibility to review individual performance and the individual's contribution as a team member. If the result of the review is that a change is needed, there will need to be some negotiation with the major shareholder and this adds a complication. It is another problem to be solved!

This is another good opportunity to remind readers that the laws governing the responsibilities of directors generally do not differentiate between different classifications or titles of director, all have the same obligations.

THE PROCESS OF LEAVING

When, for whatever reason, a director decides to resign from the Board, generally it is better 'that it were done quickly', although it is not unusual for the chairman to ask the director to continue to serve until a replacement can be found.

Retiring from the Board of a small company can need care and thought. It may not be easy to find a replacement with the attributes needed and the personality to work with a small team. It is worthwhile a director flagging their intention to retire from the Board as early as possible to the chairman, perhaps at the regular review meeting.

Retiring in mid-term, i.e. between Annual General Meetings, does not usually cause a problem because a company's Articles of Association will permit a director to be appointed to the Board to fill a 'casual vacancy'. The new director will serve until the next Annual General Meeting, offer their resignation at the meeting and simultaneously offer themselves for election by the shareholders.

If a director is retiring from a public company it will probably be necessary to advise the Stock Exchange and make a press announcement. Stock exchanges seem to be particularly interested in the retirement of an independent non-executive director.

Re-election
There is a routine 'retirement' of directors. Frequently a company's Articles of Association require that any director appointed during the year resign at the Annual General Meeting following their appointment, but they may offer themselves for re-election. In addition, after a number of years of service on the Board – frequently three, but specified in the Articles of Association – a director will have to retire. They can then offer themselves for re-election at the Annual General Meeting.

Re-election tends to be a formality, but it does give the shareholders a chance to exercise some control and vote for individual directors. It also gives a director a good chance to re-confirm they want to continue to serve the company and are confident they are able to contribute.

What to do with company documents
When retiring from the Board, you should take the chance to clear out all your files of Board papers and minutes relating to the company.

In some jurisdictions all Board papers legally remain the property of the company, not the director. If the law does not give any guidance the chairman should rule whether the papers and files should be returned to the company secretary or destroyed by the director. The retiring director will not have any further use for the papers. Accidentally leaking any of the information received from the company could be very embarrassing.

> **I have heard of a major public company that requires each director leave behind in the boardroom all papers they have received for the Board meeting so that the company secretary can destroy them. Directors then do not have any files to worry about!**

If you are worried about questions arising after you leave the Board, the company secretary is responsible for keeping a complete file of all Board papers and minutes. There is always a reference point.

Compensation

A director leaving the Board, whether voluntarily or kicking and screaming, is not usually entitled to any compensation for loss of office. If it is proposed to pay some compensation or a 'thank you', any amount must be agreed in advance by the shareholders.

Once retired from the Board the ex-director can reflect on what benefits the directorship has brought.

Tangibly, fees will have been earned. There is the possibility that the value of any shares held in the company will have increased.

Probably the greatest pleasure will come from having 'added value'; from helping a company develop and overcome obstacles to meeting long-term goals. There can be particular satisfaction in helping a small company.

Of course, you will have increased your own knowledge of business and people.

SUMMARY

◆ No director has a job for life.

◆ A director should leave a Board at the right time.

◆ The operation of each Board and performance of each director should be assessed regularly.

◆ Old files must be dealt with.

FINALLY

I have found being a director is a satisfying job and have enjoyed it, if sometimes in retrospect !

This book has taken you through the basics of the trade of 'directorship' – from the first idea of becoming a director to retirement. However, a director's education does not end with the basics, there is more to learn and directors should have a programme to continue their education.

Companies are major contributors to national prosperity and directors guide them – a great experience and a great responsibility.

Further Reading

Accounting for Growth, Terry Smith
Business Ethics – Facing the Issues, Economists Books
Directors' Dilemma's, Patrick Dunne
Fair Shares, Jonathan Charkham and Anne Simpson
Financial Management and Policy, James C. Van Horne
Financial Markets and Corporate Strategy, Grinblatt and Titman
Options, Futures and Other Derivatives, 5th edn, John C. Hall
Planning to Succeed in Business, David Erwin
Risk Financing, 2nd edn, Dr A. Gordon
Risk Management Systems, Martin Gorrod
Spicer and Pegler's Bookkeeping and Accounts
Successful Cash Management in Your Business, Richard Lehmbeck
The Effective Use of Statistics, Tim Hannagan
The Fish Rots from the Head, Bob Garratt
Understanding Corporate Strategy, John Thompson

Useful Contacts

Institutes of Directors round the world issue Guidelines also Best Practice Guidelines for directors. It is helpful to monitor the publications of institutes in other countries in addition to your national institute. No country has a monopoly on good governance and it is useful to know what is happening in other countries. Almost every country has its own institute of directors. A selection of contacts is:

Australian Institute of Company Directors, Level 25, 264–278 George Street, Sydney NSW 2000, Australia. Tel: +61 (0)2 8248 6600. Fax: +61 (0)2 8248 6633. *www.companydirectors.com.au*

Commonwealth Association for Corporate Governance, PO Box 34, Havelock, Marlborough, New Zealand.
www.cbc.to   www.combinet.net
www.ecgn.org   www.edgevantage.com

Institute of Directors, 116 Pall Mall, London SW1Y 5ED, United Kingdom. Tel: +44(0)20 7839 1233. *www.iod.com*

Institute of Directors in New Zealand, Level 2, 88 The Terrace, PO Box 8017, Wellington, New Zealand. Tel: +64 (0)4 499 0076. Fax: +64 (0)4 499 9488. *www.iod.org.nz*

The Hong Kong Institute of Directors, Room 505, Bank of America Tower, 12 Harcourt Road, Central Hong Kong. Tel: +852 2867 1185. Fax: +852 2537 9093. *www.hkiod.com*

Index

If you want to know how...

- To buy a home in the sun, and let it out
- To move overseas, and work well with the people who live there
- To get the job you want, in the career you like
- To plan a wedding, and make the Best Man's speech
- To build your own home, or manage a conversion
- To buy and sell houses, and make money from doing so
- To gain new skills and learning, at a later time in life
- To empower yourself, and improve your lifestyle
- To start your own business, and run it profitably
- To prepare for your retirement, and generate a pension
- To improve your English, or write a PhD
- To be a more effective manager, and a good communicator
- To write a book, and get it published

If you want to know how to do all these things and much, much more...

howtobooks

If you want to know how...to resolve conflict in the workplace

Margaret and Shay McConnon show you how to manage disagreements and develop trust and understanding. They enable us to begin meeting our needs and those of the other person, while maintaining the relationship and resolving our differences respectfully.

Resolving Conflict
Shay and Margaret McConnon

'One of the best books I have read on conflict resolution in my 30 + years in the field.' – Mediation Office The World Bank

ISBN 1 85703 944 0

If you want to know how...to write a report

'In this book you will learn how to write reports that will be read without unnecessary delay; understood without undue effort; accepted and, where applicable, acted upon. To achieve these aims you must do more than present all the relevant facts accurately, you must also communicate in a way that is both acceptable and intelligible to your readers.'

John Bowden

Writing a Report
John Bowden

'What is special about the text is that it is more than just how to "write reports"; it gives that extra really powerful information that can, and often does, make a difference. It is by far the most informative text covering report writing that I have seen...This book would be a valuable resource to any practising manager' – *Training Journal*

ISBN 1 85703 922 X

If you want to know how . . .to speak successfully as a manager

'Given the apprehension many people feel at the thought of public speaking, looking for a little guidance is only sensible. This book is designed to help you whether you face having to speak for the first time or if you have both some experience and proven competence. It contains information, advice and useful quotations that will extend your confidence for any speaking task. I wish I had something like this many years ago when I first stared to speak and present in public. As will become clear as you read on, success on your feet is not a matter of good luck, so I will not wish you that but I wish you well with whatever presentations you find yourself undertaking.'

Patrick Forsyth

The Management Speaker's Handbook
Templates, ideas and sample material that will transform every speaking occasion
Patrick Forsyth

'. . . a book which simply and effectively guides the reader through the preparation of a speech as well as understanding the benefits of using good notes and effective use of visual aids . . .This book will be invaluable to anyone having to speak out on a regular basis for the first time, as well as an invaluable reference for someone looking to brush up their speaking skills.' – *Profit Magazine*

'His book is unique in that it not only offers concise and practical advice on choosing content and improving technique, but it goes on to provide specific guidance in the form of blueprints of over 25 individual speaking situations. It can't get any easier.' – *Building Engineer*

ISBN 1 85703 813 4

If you want to know how...to communicate effectively with other cultures

'Doing business in another country is much more than flying out, staying in a posh hotel and eating different food. It's entering a different world, and you need to learn the rules. For that you need patience, preparation, an open mind and this book.'

Phillip Khan-Panni & Deborah Swallow

Communicating Across Cultures
Phillip Khan-Panni & Deborah Swallow

'A highly accessible and useful book that explains how to communicate with people of other nationalities. More than a book about body language, it explains how culture, values, awareness, respect and flexibility allow us to communicate effectively and without offence.' – *Weekly Telegraph*

'An excellent general introduction to communicating internationally. I particularly like the 10 top tips the authors give for each country.' – James Furnival, *The Bookseller*

ISBN 1 85703 799 5

If you want to know how...to be an effective mentor

'Mentoring is an exclusive one-to-one relationship, is completely confidential and can be a useful complement to other staff development tools. This book explains what mentoring is...and what it is not! It takes you stage by stage through the process and shows how it can be of benefit to and an opportunity for development, both for the person being mentored and for the mentor.'

David Kay and Roger Hinds

A Practical Guide to Mentoring
David Kay and Roger Hinds

'This book works through the process easily with simple steps and practical guidance, aided by an easy-to-follow contents section...A handy and quick reference text for mentors.' – *Training Journal*

ISBN 1 85703 812 6

How To Books are available through all good bookshops, or you can order direct from us through Grantham Book Services.

Tel: +44 (0)1476 541080
Fax: +44 (0)1476 541061
Email: orders@gbs.tbs-ltd.co.uk

Or via our website

www.howtobooks.co.uk

To order via any of these methods please quote the title(s) of the book(s) and your credit card number together with its expiry date.

For further information about our books and catalogue, please contact:

How To Books
3 Newtec Place
Magdalen Road
Oxford OX4 1RE

Visit our web site at

www.howtobooks.co.uk

Or you can contact us by email at info@howtobooks.co.uk